THE
FINANCIAL
GUIDE FOR
THE SINGLE
PARENT

Workbook

CHERI FULLER

Cheri Fuller is a dynamic and encouraging speaker and writer on issues relating to the family, women, children, and learning. She has been a contributor to *Focus on the Family*, *Family Circle*, *Moody*, and many other magazines and is a contributing editor to *Today's Christian Woman*. The author of fourteen books, Cheri speaks frequently at women's retreats and parent and teacher groups. She is the mother of three grown children and lives with her husband Holmes in Oklahoma City.

BRENDA ARMSTRONG

Brenda Armstrong, a single mother, is the director of CFC's single parent ministry. She has directed promotion and public affairs, produced programs for television, developed and hosted the area's first radio program for single adults for WFCJ radio, Dayton, Ohio, and founded an association of singles leaders. Brenda has shared her testimony and expertise with a variety of groups, on radio, and on local and a national television. She has written on single parent issues for several publications, including CFC's *Money Matters* and *Counselor's Corner*, Focus on the Family's *Single-Parent Family* magazine, and *SAM journal*, a publication for single adult ministry leaders. Brenda has two grown children, a grandson, and lives in Cumming, Georgia.

THE
FINANCIAL
GUIDE FOR
THE SINGLE
PARENT

from the materials
and works of

Larry
Burkett

Workbook

with Cheri Fuller
and Brenda Armstrong

MOODY PRESS
CHICAGO

All Scripture quotations are from the *New American Standard Bible*, © the Lockman Foundation
1960, 1962, 1963, 1968, 1971, 1972, 1973, 1975, 1977. Used by permission.

Edited by Adeline Griffith, Christian Financial Concepts

Library of Congress Cataloging-in-Publication Data

Burkett, Larry.
The financial guide for the single parent workbook

ISBN#0-8024-2739-1
    1. Single parents—United States—Finance, Personal.
    2. Women—United States—Finance, Personal.
      I. Title.

1 3 5 7 9 10 8 6 4 2

Printed in the United States of America.

ACKNOWLEDGMENTS

I want to thank the people who made this workbook a reality.

Special thanks to Cheri Fuller, my co-author, for her research, her efforts compiling surveys and letters from single parents, and her writing skills.

Brenda Armstrong, Christian Financial Concepts' director of single parents ministries, gave invaluable assistance, a product of her years as a single parent and working with single parents.

I greatly appreciate my editor, Adeline Griffith, for applying her expertise to the book.

Thanks also to Steve Humphrey for his helpful counsel and assistance with the cases studies.

Lee Ellis of Career Pathways furnished valuable input and information on career direction for single parents.

And to the many single parents who wrote and shared information, suggestions, and experiences, we are deeply grateful.

Larry Burkett

CONTENTS

INTRODUCTION

Financial issues usually are emotional concerns for single parents. Many don't really want to look too closely at the reality of their situations, because that could be frightening. Often, they think they don't have enough money to budget so why should they bother; and, even if they did have enough money, they wouldn't know how to begin to budget.

What most single parents don't realize is that they are not alone in their struggles. There are almost 10 million homes headed by single mothers and 1.6 million homes headed by single fathers. One in three families with children is headed by a single parent.

Setting financial goals seems wishful for many single parents. Take a moment to consider your financial goals. By writing down your current situation and establishing some goals—even small ones—you will gain a better perspective of your needs and possibly new hope of being able to manage your finances. God will honor your efforts to manage your money His way.

Single parents told us their goals:
- Providing for their children's needs.
- Getting out of debt and staying out of debt.

And the overwhelming, number one goal:
- Being able to live within their means.

To live within your means may seem impossible, but it simply means to spend no more than you make on a monthly basis. Ideally, that means to live on a cash basis and not use credit or borrowed money to provide normal living expenses. However, with incomes half that of the average two-parent family, single parents face a much greater challenge. Single mothers have the greatest challenge financially because their earning power is less than that of single dads. In fact, some of the best examples of poverty can be found in single-mother homes.

Even though their income is higher, many custodial dads have similar difficulties living on one income while raising children. The income or child care the mother may have provided is no longer there, and most dads receive little or no child support. Even parents who are supporting their children but do not live with them face financial difficulties because they have two households to support.

In addition, the obstacles to a balanced budget are numerous. Besides a reduced income, often there is debt and/or legal expenses resulting from a divorce. There's the child-care dilemma, little or no child support, problems with home and auto repair, and the time crunch for single parents rearing children alone while working a full-time job and struggling to make ends meet.

Nevertheless, the goal of financial freedom is not an impossible one, even for the single parent. The church has a great opportunity to be God's hand extended in healing and restoration for the single parent family. Those in the body of Christ are instructed in God's Word to take care of one another; and God makes His heart abundantly clear when it comes to those in need (His Word specifically mentions widows and orphans).

If God's principles are followed, and if the local church assists these families, as Scripture directs, the single parent family can have a healthy financial life and even build a surplus to share with others in need.

Many unsaved and unchurched single parents will be turning to the church if the government continues to cut welfare benefits and single parents continue to earn less than poverty levels in income. The working poor have been the hardest hit, and many more will be joining their ranks as benefits disappear.

For the majority of low-income, working single parents, ongoing support is just not available—not through the government and, unfortunately, not through the church. However, as the church becomes more familiar with the real needs of single parents, many more churches will offer ongoing support.

Even if your church does not recognize the need to support single parent families, you can still find answers. *One is through a personal relationship with Jesus Christ.* He has promised to meet all your needs and, often, He does that miraculously as you release your needs to Him.

The material in this workbook covers many of the most common financial difficulties faced by single parents. Most of the examples given represent custodial mothers, not only because their number is much greater than that of custodial single fathers, but also because our counseling has shown that this group is more likely to seek financial help and support; and, their financial difficulties are usually more severe. However, we believe that all single parents (male as well as female) can benefit from the examples we are giving, so we have kept the references generic when not relating actual circumstances.

No matter what situations lead single parents to seek help, the church has a God-given opportunity to offer direction, forgiveness, healing, support, and restoration—by building relationships with them and showing God's love to them in a tangible way.

GETTING STARTED

This workbook will provide some practical guidelines, steps to budgeting, and money-saving strategies. The book was designed to accompany and complement *The Financial Guide for the Single Parent*, originally published as *The Complete Financial Guide for Single Parents*. Whether you are doing the workbook with a Christian Financial Concepts (CFC) referral counselor, in a group, or sitting at your desk or kitchen table working through it alone, get your pen, get ready, and remember, God knows the plans He has for you and your children—plans for a future and a hope, not calamity. (See Jeremiah 29:11.) He says that when we seek Him with all our hearts, we will find Him.

You've made the first step by opening this workbook. Let's get started finding His ways for managing money!

Where You Begin

If you are seeking financial counseling you must have goals in mind. You may be seeking help because you are in a crisis.

NEVER GIVE UP!

Finances can be overwhelming, so I've learned to start slowly, start somewhere, and tackle one thing at a time! During World War II, one of Winston Churchill's advisors told him, "Never give up, never, never, never, give up."

I applied that principle to my finances at one of the lowest times in my life. I found the job is too big, the task too awesome not to *let go and let God*; His yoke is easy and His burden is light.

I feel like I am more financially secure now than I have ever been in my life, including when I was married. I may never be independently wealthy, but we have what we need, some of what we want, some to give to others, and I don't have to worry about tomorrow: God's already there.

— Connie Dady
Warrensburg, Missouri

Your crisis may be any number of things. Put a check mark by the ones that apply to you and if yours is not listed here, add it (them).

- lack of housing   _____
- past due rent or utilities   _____
- threat of repossession (car or belongings)   _____
- low or no child support payments   _____
- sudden income drop   _____
- other _____

_____

Your financial goals may include some of the following. Put a check mark by the ones that apply to you. If yours is not listed, add it (them).

- finding answers to my immediate crisis   _____
- increasing my income   _____
- paring down expenses   _____
- addressing long-term needs   _____
- learning how to manage the money I have   _____
- other _____

_____

Action Point

Write any thoughts or plans you have concerning your financial goals.

_____

_____

_____

_____

_____

LIVING WITHIN YOUR MEANS
UNDERSTANDING WANTS, NEEDS, AND DESIRES

To work toward the goal of *living within your means,* you first must get wants, needs, and desires in their proper relationship.

Needs, Wants, and Desires: What's the Difference?

God has promised to provide your needs, not your wants or desires. Although He

14

takes your wants and desires into consideration, He only provides what is best for you. Many times you are unhappy because you don't see the difference between luxuries and necessities. The following will help you understand those differences.

NEEDS

These are the purchases necessary to provide your basic requirements, such as food, clothing, housing, medical coverage, and others.

> *"And if we have food and covering, with these we shall be content"* (1 Timothy 6:8).

WANTS

Wants involve choices about the quality of goods to be used: designer clothing versus plain, durable clothing; steak versus hamburger; a new car versus a used car. Peter gives a point of reference for determining wants in a person's life.

> *"And let not your adornment be merely external—braiding the hair, and wearing gold jewelry, or putting on dresses; but let it be the hidden person of the heart, with the imperishable quality of a gentle and quiet spirit, which is precious in the sight of God"* (1 Peter 3:3-4).

DESIRES

These are choices according to God's plan that can be made only out of surplus funds *after* all other obligations have been met. When you learn to give your wants and desires to God, He changes your perspective. When you begin desiring what He wants for you, He often supplies much more than you need.

> *"Do not love the world, nor the things in the world. If anyone loves the world, the love of the Father is not in him. For all that is in the world, the lust of the flesh and the lust of the eyes and the boastful pride of life, is not from the Father, but is from the world"* (1 John 2:15-16).

Action Points

List your NEEDS and your children's NEEDS

_____

_____

_____

_____

List your family's WANTS.

_____

_____

_____

_____

List your family's DESIRES.

_____

_____

_____

_____

THE DIVISIONS OF INCOME

1. God's part: The word _tithe_ means one-tenth. It is the _minimum_ portion that a Christian should give to God. (In the Bible, people usually gave much more than 10 percent of their income or harvest.) The tithe's purpose is to be a testimony of God's ownership of everything. We, as good stewards (or managers), give back to Him a small portion of what we have. It is a personal act.

The _first_ part of your income belongs to God. A verse in Proverbs says that God has asked for our first fruits: the first and best of all we receive. It is only by honoring the Lord from the first part of all we have that God can take control.

"_Honor the Lord from your wealth, and from the first of all your produce; so your barns will be filled with plenty, and your vats will overflow with new wine_" (Proverbs 3:9-10).

2. Government's part: There's a legitimate role in God's Word for government, and we should honor the authority that God has put above us. The taxes we owe the government should be paid.

"_Then He said to them, 'Then render to Caesar the things that are Caesar's; and to God the things that are God's'_" (Matthew 22:21).

> **The portion available after tithe and taxes are paid is called *NET SPENDABLE INCOME*.**

3. Your part: God commands us to provide for our families (housing, food, clothing, and so on). If you are a noncustodial or joint custody parent and you are required to pay child support, those payments should be your next priority.

> *"If any one does not provide for his own, and especially for those of his household, he has denied the faith, and is worse than an unbeliever"* (1 Timothy 5:8).

4. Creditors' part: God says you should pay your debts.

> *"The wicked borrows and does not pay back, but the righteous is gracious and gives"* (Psalm 37:21).

5. Others part: Faithful management over a period of time will yield a fifth portion—a surplus—which means you may have more than you need. This is a major goal for any Christian. It is the surplus that allows you to respond to the needs of others, and it provides the flexibility to meet emergencies without credit.

> *"At this present time your abundance being a supply for their want, that their abundance also may become a supply for your want, that there may be equality"* (2 Corinthians 8:14).

When considering the five divisions of income, you may have some emotional conflict as a single parent. You may fear there will not be enough money to go around; you may think you are a failure if you can't provide for your family's needs yourself. However, you must pray, set priorities, and trust God to provide.

WHERE ARE YOU?

Starting a budget is just like starting on a trip. You cannot set a course without first determining where you are. Let's start by figuring your Net Spendable Income (how much you have left to spend on your needs after tithe and taxes) and your present level of spending. You will need a sheet of paper and a copy of Form 1 from the Appendix.

Action Points

Step 1: Figure your gross income per month. Divide annual amounts by twelve for monthly average.

a. Income   _____

This includes salary, wages, tips, commissions, bonuses, self-employment income, alimony, child support, public assistance, rent subsidy, Social Security, disability, tax refunds, veteran's or retirement benefits. Note: Figure amounts on income before taxes are deducted. For irregular income, average several low income months.

b. Interest   _____

This includes checking or savings account interest.

c. Dividends   _____

This is any money you receive from investments.

d. Other

    This includes food stamps, regular money gifts—anything not added in "income."

GROSS INCOME PER MONTH (total of a through d) _____

Step 2: Figure your Net Spendable Income per month. Now subtract the following from your *gross income.*

a. Tithe _____

    This is money you are currently giving to God.

b. Taxes _____

    This includes federal, state, local, Social Security, FICA, or self-employment taxes. <u>Note</u>: If you pay self-employment taxes quarterly, divide the amount by three or, if yearly, by twelve to get the monthly amount.)

NET SPENDABLE INCOME (results after deducting tithes and taxes) _____

> <u>*Note:*</u> **Business expense reimbursements should not be considered family income. Avoid the trap of using expense money to buffer family spending or the result will be an indebtedness that cannot be paid.**

Step 3: Know what you spend. To figure the amount you are currently spending, you must know your *fixed expenses* and your *variable expenses. Fixed expenses* are those that do not change from month to month. *Variable expenses* are those that may change from month to month or are not due every month. The following will help you figure both kinds of expenses.

Fixed Expenses

- **Housing Expenses**—All monthly expenses necessary to operate the home, including taxes, insurance, maintenance, and utilities. The amount used for utility payments should be an average monthly amount for the past twelve months.
- **Automobile Expenses**—Includes payments, insurance, gas, oil, maintenance (repairs), and depreciation (money put aside to replace the car).

Variable Expenses

- **Auto Expenses**—Regular maintenance and repairs.
- **Food**—All grocery expenses, including paper goods and non-food products normally purchased at grocery stores. Include milk, bread, and items purchased in addition to regular shopping trips, but do not include eating-out expenses.
- **Outstanding Debts**—Includes all monthly payments on credit cards, loans, or other obligations, except home mortgage and auto payments.
- **Utilities**—See above in Housing Expenses category.
- **Insurance**—Includes payments for health, life, disability, or any insurance not associated with the home or auto.
- **Entertainment/Recreation**—Includes money spent on vacations, eating out, camping trips, club dues, sporting equipment, hobby expenses, and athletic events. Don't forget Little League expense, booster clubs, and the like.
- **Clothing**—The average annual amount spent on clothes for your family divided by twelve.
- **Medical Expenses**—Includes insurance deductibles (the amount that you must pay per year on your medical bills before some insurance benefits begin), doctors' bills, co-pays per office visit, sliding scale fees, treatments, tests, eye exams and glasses, prescriptions, or dental work or orthodontic treatments. Add only the amounts you actually pay that are not reimbursed. Divide the annual amount by twelve for the monthly amounts.
- **Savings**—Every family should allocate something for savings, no matter how small.
- **Miscellaneous**—Specific expenses that do not seem to fit anywhere else; pocket allowance (coffee money), miscellaneous gifts, Christmas presents, toiletries, haircuts.
- **School/Child Care**—This is the amount you spend for child care; preschool; after-school care; or tuition for private schools, technical schools, or colleges. Include related expenses, such as field trips, snacks, and so on. Remember, if you figure the amount on what you spend each year, divide that figure by twelve for your monthly cost. All other categories will have to be reduced to provide these funds.

Two Ways to Determine Expenditures (what you spend)

- Go through your checkbook for the previous year and divide your spending into the categories listed on Form 1 in the Appendix.
- Keep a diary for at least one month, listing everything you buy by category. Include any expenses that are not paid every month, such as car repairs and clothes.

Step 4: Compare income versus expenses. If total income exceeds total expenses, you will only have to implement a method of budget control in your home. If expenses exceed income, examine each spending category to discover what adjustments can be made. You may find that it will be necessary to make lifestyle changes.

In the following pages, we will suggest ideas used by many single parents that can help you cut expenses and budget better in each category and help you deal with the pitfalls that prevent a "balanced budget."

EVERYBODY NEEDS A BUDGET!

The Bible says that a borrower is a slave to the lender. If you are not able to pay your debts according to your agreements because of lack of money or over-spending, you are in financial bondage. However, true financial freedom comes from learning to become a good *steward*. A steward cares for something that belongs to someone else. Since everything you have really belongs to God, being a good steward means managing well the money God has entrusted to you. It is possible, even if your income is low, but it's only possible if you look at your situation realistically and *plan ahead*.

A good spending plan, or budget, requires *action* and *discipline* to make it work. It may require sacrifice. Remember, if we fail to plan we are *planning to fail*. So begin the planning now!

Be patient and remember that budgeting is a *process*, and it can take up to nine months to a year to get on and maintain a budget completely.

> <u>*Note:*</u> **The examples given may not address every situation or financial need you face as a single parent, but they do represent some of the more common difficulties experienced by lower-income custodial single parents. However, all single parents will benefit from the many suggestions throughout this workbook.**

Chapter 3

THE WELFARE SYSTEM

Although most single parents say they don't really make enough money to budget, it's especially true for families with very low incomes. Most of them want to provide for their families, but the struggle to make ends meet is a daily battle with few solutions. Frustrations can lead to:

- Drug and alcohol abuse.
- Child endangerment or abuse.
- Compromise in values and standards.
- A poverty mentality that is passed down through family generations.

The government isn't the solution. Even with recent changes the system doesn't encourage independence. Welfare is bondage. The government decides the following:

- Whether or not you will work outside the home.
- How much you can earn.
- How many hours you can work.
- Where you can take your child for child care.
- How much your home can be worth.
- How much you can save.
- How much your car can be worth.
- If you can obtain job training or go to college.

The struggle to break free defeats many who try. Many people believe that all a single parent needs to do to avoid being needy is to get a job. That simply is not true. The disadvantages for the welfare recipients who work keeps them stuck in the system.

To leave the welfare system, you lose several things:

- Your monthly check.
- Food stamp benefits.
- Medicaid for you and your children, even if the new job does not provide it.
- Day care after the first year.
- Subsidized housing, if you have it.

On an entry level income, you cannot replace those benefits, so the temptation is to give up and return to the system. However, when you consider the bondage it causes, it's worth it to break free. You need guidance and support to get along without welfare.

I don't believe people, especially Christians, should have to look to the government to meet their needs. Suggestions for how the church can help single parents are given in Chapter 11.

The following are some suggestions that worked for other single parents.

- Pray for your specific needs. God has promised to be a husband to the husbandless and a father to the fatherless. You can be honest with Him about your needs.
- Ask your family for help. God's Word says families should provide for their own first. That includes your immediate family and the children's other parent.
- Ask your church for help. Be specific. Help to educate them about single parent needs.
- If you must use government assistance, determine to get off and stay off as soon as possible.
- Set educational goals if needed.
- Remember that God wants you to depend on Him, not the government. He will provide for your needs.
- Enlist prayer support and establish accountability relationships with key people.
- Work with a trained budget counselor or another single parent experienced in overcoming your obstacles.
- Take a step. God will meet you where you are.
- Remember that God has a plan for your life. He created you for a purpose.
- Begin tithing something if you're not already doing so.

Action Point

Write your plan for "no more government assistance."

_____

_____

_____

_____

_____

_____

Others have broken free, and so can you. It starts in the attitude of your heart.

The suggestions in the rest of this workbook and in _The Financial Guide for the Single Parent_ book will help you to stretch your limited funds.

Chapter 4

FINANCIAL PITFALLS AND HOW TO DEAL WITH THEM

When you start on a journey, it's helpful to know what obstacles you are going to face. That way, you're prepared for them and they don't derail you from your goals or cause a collision. In the same way, there are pitfalls that are particularly prevalent for single parents.

Pitfalls to Avoid

• DEBT. Don't use charge cards to subsidize your income.

• SHOPPING WHEN DEPRESSED. If you purchase things on credit you get even more depressed when the bills come.

• INADEQUATE CHILD SUPPORT. The expectation of child-support payments from the former spouse is often shattered; approximately 50 percent of child support is never paid.

TRUSTING GOD WITH FINANCES

When Charles experienced a divorce, he was granted custody of his little boy. But he faced many struggles: feeling the emotional jolt of grief, trying to deal with the reality of his situation, finding child care, and being embarrassed to ask for help.

Even with his income as a medical clerk and the child support from his former wife, he had hard choices to make each month because he and his young son had only about $100 left after paying for housing, child care, and auto expenses. But with planning, the help of family and a few friends, and trust in God, they have made it.

"As I look back over the last five years, I am amazed at how the Lord provided for us," says Charles. "There is no way we should have survived those first few years, considering our income and expenses, but God always provided in one area so the funds would be available in another area."

The most important thing Charles says he learned early in life, and found to be so true during the challenges of single parenting, was to plan his budget and to tithe. "Even if the amount was meager, God was and continues to be faithful to provide our needs as we put Him first," he says.

- GIVING IN TO THE "GIMMIES." When your kids' wants exceed your budget and you have a hard time saying, "No," you've hit a roadblock.

- TRYING TO MAINTAIN A HIGHER STANDARD OF LIVING. This includes living in the same house, having the kids do the same after-school activities and lessons, and having the same shopping and spending habits they had when the other parent was in the home.

- UNEXPECTED EXPENSES. These are auto or home appliance repair or unexpected medical expenses.

- BEING AFRAID OR EMBARRASSED TO ASK FOR HELP. You deprive the church of opportunities to fulfill its biblical responsibility if you conceal your need.

- CHANGE IN MEDICAL BENEFITS. Often health-care concerns override all others in determining whether someone stays on welfare or goes to work.

Having a low income means making choices: pay the phone bill or the gas bill? buy cough medicine or snow boots? In hard times, health insurance is a luxury, and without it you may be robbed of your peace of mind.

The following telephone numbers are provided for your own research into alternate health plans. Brotherhood Newsletter, 800-269-4030; Christian Care Ministry, 800-374-2562; All Saints, 800-259-0095; and Good Samaritan, 317-861-1424.

Action Point

Discover Your Pitfalls

What's your biggest financial pitfall? Different things trip up different people. For one parent, it was clothing. "I would walk into a clothing store and blow my budget." For another it was Christmas and birthday gifts.

Write your pitfalls here.

_____

_____

_____

_____

> *"Offer to God a sacrifice of thanksgiving, and pay your vows to the Most High; and call upon Me in the day of trouble; I shall rescue you, and you will honor Me"* (Psalm 50:14-15).

In many situations I've seen, in which repayment of debts seemed impossible, once the individual made an absolute commitment to pay what was legitimately due, God provided the means to do so.

So you do your part and God will do His part! It won't always be an instantaneous solution, but the old adage is still true: God is rarely early, but never late. And He is always faithful.

For example, one single mother was losing her house to the county sheriff's auction for delinquent property taxes, which she knew nothing about when her husband walked out and failed to provide. But, God miraculously intervened by providing her a job with the county to "work off her taxes."

This job utilized her computer skills and also qualified as an internship that would give her college credit required for her degree. The local television station asked to do a story on her family, and the local newspaper followed suit. God not only provided but also went beyond all she could think or ask. He allowed her family to keep their house. And her bosses were so impressed with her work skills that she was offered a permanent full-time job with the county as an assistant program director.

Hidden Debts

A common error is to overlook non-monthly debts such as doctor bills, family loans, bank notes, repairs, and other occasional expenses. Thus, when payments come due, there is no money to pay for them.

To avoid unpleasant surprises, establish and maintain a list of debts in total. The list must be reviewed and updated on a regular basis, and funds must be set aside in the budget to make the necessary payments. Make a copy of Form 8 in the Appendix to list your debts.

THE SHOPPING PITFALL

I saw a bumper sticker recently that said, "When things get tough, the tough go shopping." It's meant to promote a philosophy of handling stress and tough times through shopping, but that will land you right in credit card disaster! It would be more accurate to say the tough *don't* go shopping, because it takes less effort to shop and spend than it does to refrain from shopping and spending.

Although shopping can serve as a temporary mood-lifter when you're down, the consequences on your budget are even more depressing. There's a better way. The first step is to control impulse spending.

Impulse items are unnecessary purchases made on the spur-of-the-moment.

Excuses for buying:

- It was on sale.
- I just couldn't resist it.
- I owe it to myself or my kids.

In order to consider every purchase in light of the budget and control impulse spending using an "Impulse Buying Sheet" like the one in Figure 4.1. Create your own.

1. List the item you want to buy.
2. Wait thirty days before buying.
3. Compare prices and list cost and store on sheet.
4. Purchase after thirty days if funds are available without upsetting your budget.
5. If funds are still not available, save for the item.

IMPULSE LIST				
DATE	IMPULSE ITEM	1	2	3

FIGURE 4.1

You also can deal with the "splurge urge" by doing the following.

 Leave your checkbook and/or credit card at home when you go out and carry only enough cash to meet your anticipated needs for the day. That gives you time to really think about the purchase before going back to the store.

 Avoid tempting places like malls, gift shops, hobby or sporting goods stores, television shopping channels, and irresistible mail order catalogs.

 Use self-discipline. As one single parent says, "Making ends meet takes a lot of saying no to things, especially recreational shopping!"

Action Point

What are the impulse items you are most tempted to buy?

_____

_____

_____

What are the steps you will take this month to avoid impulse spending?

_____

_____

_____

_____

_____

_____

GIFTS

A major budget-buster for many single parents is overspending on gifts. Tradition encourages us to purchase a gift for nearly every occasion. Unfortunately, the net result is often a gift someone else doesn't want or need, purchased with money that was needed for something else.

Many times the cost is higher because the gift is bought at the last minute. If gifts are a part of normal spending, budget for them and buy ahead—reasonably.

To bring the cost of gifts under control, consider the following steps.

1. Keep an event calendar for the year and plan ahead.
2. Determine not to buy any gifts on credit (especially Christmas gifts).
3. Initiate crafts within the family and make some of the needed gifts.
4. Draw family names for selected gifts rather than giving to everyone.
5. Make and give "gifts of time" or "promise" coupons for friends and loved ones. Each coupon offers recipients services or something they would enjoy, such as doing their household chores for a day, providing a few hours of baby-sitting for a special occasion, providing breakfast in bed for a family member, or taking the kids to the zoo or a museum. This kind of gift continues to give after the special day and costs less than purchased gifts.

If you are a low-income parent, you may be tempted to let some expenses go unpaid, rather than allow your children to do without. Or you may continue to purchase gifts for them even when it's not a special occasion, because of your guilt or their lack. Learn to place the desire to give to your children in God's hands; He wants to show you how to give good gifts. The following will help you prepare for gift purchases.

- Pray about the special day well in advance, and ask God for guidance.
- Make the gift special. If you buy a gift, avoid instant gratification. Don't buy a popular or expensive item on the spur of the moment. Instead, choose an item your child has desired consistently for a long time.
- Tell your child to ask God if he or she should have it. Avoid saying you can't buy

something because you don't have the money. Avoid thinking it too. God has a way of supplying anything if He wants your child to have it.

- Start saving any extra money that comes in, and add one or two dollars a week toward the item.

- When you have enough, watch for the item to go on sale and buy it, even if the event is still six months away.

Another problem is that of your younger children buying for you, especially if the other parent isn't around or doesn't want to help them shop. You may not be able to afford to give your children much money, and finding someone to shop with them is difficult. The following suggestions may work for you.

- Some department stores and organizations provide Secret-Santa-type stores. Inexpensive items are arranged in a special room where workers help children select gifts while parents wait outside. Prices are usually low, and children get to shop by themselves.

- Through schools, scouts, churches, and other organizations, children often have the opportunity to make gifts for their parents. These gifts can be special treasures.

- Friends or church members can help by taking the child shopping.

THE CHILD SUPPORT PITFALL

Even though you will find no biblical basis for taking your former spouse to court for non-payment of alimony, the issue of child support is an entirely different matter. Unlike the parents, children have no choice in their circumstances. They did not choose to be born; they were given into your care by God. Parents' responsibility to support their children doesn't end when a marriage or relationship ends. Parents can't skip out on child support simply because it is inconvenient.

As Paul said in 1 Timothy 5:8, "*But if anyone does not provide for his own, and especially for those of his household, he has denied the faith, and is worse than an unbeliever.*"

The final decision of whether to sue must be made prayerfully and on the basis of actual need—not anger or greed. And be certain that you have exhausted all other means of negotiating before appealing to the courts for assistance.

- Be sure and get godly counsel. *"Without consultation, plans are frustrated, but with many counselors they succeed"* (Proverbs 15:22).

- Contact the Association for Children for Enforcement of Support (ACES), a nonprofit, self-help organization that has assisted thousands of people in locating and collecting child support. You can call them at 800-537-7072.

DEALING WITH THE "GIMMIES"

A single dad gives some excellent advice concerning children—from his experience as both the custodial and noncustodial parent.

- *Never try to buy your children's affection.* Trying to play a game of one-upmanship with your child's other parent is a losing battle.

- *Don't try to make up for the absence of the noncustodial parent by indulging in unwarranted spending for unnecessary items.* Try to impart values to your children by talking to them about what is really valuable in life.

- *When you tithe to your church, be sure your children know that you tithe and why you do it, and involve them in the process of giving to God.* Also teach your children to put aside a tithe out of any money they receive.

- *If your children are old enough, put them on a budget of their own.* Older children can learn to manage a budget that includes their tithe, clothing, entertainment, and savings.

Action Point

The following is one thing I will do this week to help impart healthy values about money to my children.

_____

_____

_____

_____

TRYING TO KEEP UP THE PREVIOUS LIFESTYLE

Accepting the realities of your lifestyle after a loss, whether divorce, death, or separation is difficult, but the sooner you do the fewer mistakes you'll make and the less debt you'll have. Try the following suggestions.

- *Have someone sit down with you and help analyze your financial situation, especially if your income does not cover your expenses.* Be sure the person you choose has experience in budgeting.

- *Make cuts where you can.* If you have more money going out than coming in, see if there are any places to make cuts without significantly changing your lifestyle. To get ideas for cutting expenses, look at the money-saving suggestions for each category in this workbook. Would those cuts allow you to live within your income?

- *Make the hard decisions quickly.* Make decisions about changes, such as selling the house or getting a more economical car. If selling the house is what needs to happen, do it right away, before it brings on increased debt.

HOW GOD PROVIDED

My daughter began taking music lessons when she was four years old, and she showed promise from the very beginning. When her father left us, she was seven. It was a very hard decision, and many people did not understand, but I took her out of her violin lessons because I could not handle it financially or emotionally. Of course, it was extremely difficult, but I had to accept that we could not keep up the same lifestyle—and that included after-school activities. She returned to her music after a three-year absence and the long-term effects were negligible.

In fact, as a senior in high school, she was chosen first chair violinist for the Atlanta Symphony Youth Orchestra, one of the best in the nation. She was heavily recruited by several universities' music departments and is now attending a major university on a violin scholarship.

—Susan Bryg
Roswell, Georgia

Major cuts could be to move to a smaller home or an apartment, trade in the car, and/or destroy all credit cards.

Acknowledging the fact that you can't have the same lifestyle you had before is difficult, but accepting and adjusting to the limitations will make the process of financial recovery a growth experience for you and your children.

Action Point

1. Unrealistic expectations, whether of myself, my children, their other parent, or my finances, are major sources of stress. To be more realistic and to reduce stress, I will make the following adjustments or changes in my lifestyle.

Major cuts: _____

_____

_____

Minor cuts: _____

_____

_____

_____

_____

_____

2. Considering my income and obligations, the following expectations are unrealistic at this point.

_____

_____

_____

_____

_____

3. I will seek help from: (financial counselor, pastor, former spouse, family, friends, nonprofit agencies).

_____

_____

_____

_____

_____

ANTICIPATE THE UNEXPECTED

Most people don't plan for the "unexpected expenses," but the reality is that kids get sick or hurt themselves and have to go to the emergency room; cars need repairs, and appliances break down. The expenses that we're unprepared for can wreck a budget, so here are some ways to deal with them.

- *Set aside money every month for house and automobile maintenance.* Then when something breaks down you can pay for it instead of borrowing.
- *Begin an emergency fund.* If there's not enough money to set any aside for an "Emergency Fund," go back over your budget to find some way to put aside extra funds.
- *Develop a plan of action.* Find other ways to prepare for the situations that cause stress, especially if you lack a surplus. Look in your community to find a reliable, honest repair person before a breakdown occurs so you won't be at the mercy of choosing the closest mechanic or repair shop or having to get one out of the yellow pages at the last minute.

Also, think about what's going to be your recourse—family, neighbors, church—in case of an emergency. Have a backup for child care; find someone who could care for your children in case of illness or emergency.

Anticipate the emergencies and unexpected expenses, and you will eliminate a great deal of the stress when they do occur.

Action Point

Write below possible "unexpected events" and your plan of action.

_____
_____
_____
_____
_____
_____
_____
_____
_____
_____

THE PRIDE PITFALL: BEING AFRAID OR EMBARRASSED TO ASK FOR HELP

- Some Christians believe that if they have a need or can't provide for their families they're not trusting God; they feel like failures. They don't ask for help because they think all the responsibility is theirs.

- On the other hand, there are those who have become accustomed to receiving and they take no responsibility. They become dependent on others and feel little hope that anyone, including God, can change things. They don't ask because they trust more in circumstances than God or others.

- Other people don't ask because they have asked before and were refused help, and they don't want to face rejection again or be made to feel like beggars.

You and I are going to show up in heaven someday and be surprised to find out all the things God had for us that we didn't get because we didn't ask for them. (Read James 4:2.)

God has promised to meet our needs but, as I see it, in most instances He uses people to whom He has given a surplus to help the less fortunate. As the Bible says, "*If a brother or sister is without clothing and in need of daily food, and one of you says to them, 'Go in peace, be warmed and be filled'; and yet you do not give them what is necessary for their body; what use is that?*" (James 2:15-16).

The following are some guidelines for ways to ask for help.

- Believe that God wants to meet your needs.
- Believe that God uses others to meet needs.
- Be willing to receive what God wants to provide.
- Be sure you are spending the money you have wisely.
- Be sure you are living on a monthly budget. If people want to help you financially, you will be able to tell them how much you actually need.
- Be sure you are in some type of financial counseling. Many churches require that recipients of help are in financial counseling, and often the church is willing to provide it.
- Be willing to be accountable.
- Be willing to give as well as receive.

CHANGES IN MEDICAL BENEFITS

Changes in medical expenses can come from a variety of sources, and many of the changes may be out of your control. Changing jobs often creates a lack of insurance until it becomes effective in the new job. Some workers may be surprised to learn that their new low income, full-time job doesn't provide medical coverage for employees. Even if they are insured, they may find that they must pay more out-of-pocket expenses or contribute more toward insurance premiums than anticipated.

Although most government welfare programs pay for all of a child's medical expenses, single parents often are surprised that they may be required to pay part of their own expense for medical care. Even if single parents have children that are covered by the other parent's insurance through work, they may be surprised to find that they have to pay the fees or deductibles the other parent used to pay for their children's care, especially if these charges were not included in the support decree.

If you anticipate any of these expenses, you'll need to have some funds reserved in an emergency account to cover them.

SOMETHING FOR NOTHING SCAMS

Although there are more, the following list should help you learn to recognize a scam when you see one (others are listed in the chapter on home business).

1. **PRIZE OFFERS.** This is a popular scheme in which victims are let to believe, by phone or by postcard, that they have won a major prize (a car or $10,000, for example), and to receive it they have to send $500 to pay redemption fees or taxes. Unfortunately, as yet, no one has received the car or the money.

2. **ADVANCE-FEE LOANS.** People with bad credit who are deeply in debt and who can't get a loan from the bank and have an emergency, or want to consolidate debts, are prime candidates for this scam. Often solicited by phone or through advertisement in a local newspaper, you are assured a loan if you pay $200 or

$300 in advance, as a processing fee. However, once you've paid the "advance," there is no loan.

3. **FREE VACATIONS.** A single mother received a postcard congratulating her for being "approved" to receive a vacation at a resort in Mexico. The message said, "Please call to confirm within 48 hours or you'll lose your chance." Having not been able to afford a vacation for her family for several years, she jumped at the offer. When she called, however, she was asked to pay a nonrefundable $50 fee to receive her "vacation certificate." After having written and mailed the $50 check, she was informed only days before the departure date that the trip was canceled, and the firm making the offer had closed. The single mom was left $50 poorer and very disappointed.

   In other cases, people who finally do go on the "free vacation" find the room is cheap and undesirable and it cost $4000 to move to a better room. Save yourself the trouble and the loss of money.

   Also, sometimes when the initial call is made the "lucky recipient" is asked for a credit card number. Don't be foolish! Avoid this scam!

4. **REPAIR RIP-OFFS.** This scam varies from offers to repair roofs, driveways, and furnaces to fixing cracked foundations. It goes like this: A truck pulls up and the driver says, "We've been repairing roofs in this area and have some materials left over. I see your roof could use some work and since we're in the neighborhood anyway, we could do it today for half-price—only $500." One such man knocked on the door of an elderly woman, living on a fixed income, who thought she was getting a real bargain price to get her roof repaired, so she wrote a check, had the work done (in record time), and the first time it rained, tar washed down the sides of the house. Of course, the "repair" person had left town by then (he had cashed her check at a nearby store only minutes after leaving her house). She had to pay a second person to come clean the tar off the sides of the house.

5. **CHARITY CONS.** In this scam, the callers identify the charity by a name similar to a well-known national or local charity. Most of the donations, however, go into their pockets as "administrative expenses" and salaries.

6. **SNEAKY SWEEPSTAKES.** The sweepstakes promotion guarantees you will win some amount of money ($10,000 or more) if you return your entry and buy a product. Pass it up!

7. **SECURED CREDIT CARDS.** If you are offered a credit card with the stipulation of paying the processing fee of $50 or more, you are likely to be denied a card unless you can post a savings account to establish collateral. Some legitimate banks issue such secured credit cards, but avoid the independent marketing firms that charge a fee for processing (who often promise to return it if you are denied a card). Usually the victim is denied a card but, by being unable to secure the card with a savings account, also loses the $50 processing fee.

8. **RECOVER ROOM.** This scam is double trouble for victims who already have been taken, so avoid it! Fake firms (such as "ABC Recovery") or someone who poses as a government agency will call and say they know you lost money in a scam and will offer, for a $200 fee, to get it back for you. If you send the $200, you lose again.

Chapter 5

THE GUIDELINE BUDGET

A guideline budget is simply a spending plan that uses percentages to tell you how much you can reasonably spend in each category, such as Housing, Food, Clothing, Automobile, and so on. A sample percentage guideline for single parents in the median income range is on page 43. Copy Form 3 from the Appendix to figure the percentages you are currently spending in each category.

The percentages in the guideline budget show how much of an average single parent's income can be *allocated* (set aside) for each category in the budget. There are a lot of differences in family situations, income levels, and needs, so your percentages may vary from the guideline budget.

Also, your budget will vary depending on your area of the country (for example, whether state taxes are collected or if subsidized housing is available for low-income families).

PURPOSE OF A GUIDELINE

The guideline is developed to determine a standard against which you can compare present spending patterns. The guideline budget:

- Helps serve as a basis for determining areas of overspending that are creating the *greatest problems*.
- Helps determine where to make cuts and adjustments.

If you are overspending, the percentage guideline can be used as a goal for budgeting.

41

Although the percentages are guides only, and not absolutes, they do help to set a limit to spending in a particular area.

For example: A single-parent family spending 50 percent or more of their Net Spendable Income on Housing will have difficulty balancing their budget. In most single parent budgets there is little flexibility to absorb overspending on Housing or Automobiles.

GUIDELINES

The **Net Spendable Income** (determined by subtracting your tithe and taxes from your gross income) is used to calculate the ideal spending for each budget category.

In categories containing *variable* expenses, which are expenses that change from month to month or are not paid every month, average monthly figures must be added to the appropriate category. For example, if you pay your home or renter's insurance once a year, the annual amount would be divided by twelve and the resulting monthly amount would be added to the Housing category, thus raising the percentage for the Housing category.

However, the total combined allocation for Housing, Food, and Automobile cannot exceed 65 percent of your Net Spendable Income or you will find it nearly impossible to balance your budget. A balanced budget is one in which all category expenses are covered by available income. Make a copy of Form 2 in the Appendix to figure your variable expenses.

If all your expenses in categories 3 through 12 total less than 100 percent of your Net Spendable Income, you have income to provide for child care or investments. If the total is more than 100 percent of your Net Spendable Income when child care or investments are added, you have a *deficit* (a lack) and some of the other categories must be reduced to provide funds for these expenses. If these categories don't currently apply to you, or your total expenses are still less than 100 percent of your NSI after adding them, any extra money is considered *Unallocated Surplus Income* (meaning nothing is planned for it).

Each category represented on the Budget Percentage Guidelines sheet is explained in more detail in the following chapters.

BUDGET PERCENTAGE GUIDELINES

Salary for guideline = $13,000 to $14,000 per year

GROSS INCOME PER MONTH _____

1.	Tithe	10% of Gross
2.	Tax	2% to 10% of Gross[1]

NET SPENDABLE INCOME _____

3.	Housing	40%[2]
4.	Food	5%[3]
5.	Auto	15%
6.	Insurance	3%
7.	Debts (not including house/car)	4%
8.	Entertainment/Recreation	5%
9.	Clothing	5%
10.	Savings	5%
11.	Medical	5%
12.	Miscellaneous	4%
(13.)	Child Care/School/Child Support	8–15%[6]
(14.)	Investments	____[7]
(15.)	Unallocated Surplus Income	____[8]

1. State taxes are variable depending on the state in which you live. Social Security taxes are 7.65 percent. If you qualify for Earned Income Credit, due to low income, your taxes will be reduced significantly. Contact a financial counselor to help you determine what your total taxes will be.

2. This category percentage is going to vary tremendously, depending on your area of the country. Also, if you qualify for public assistance or put into action one of the housing alternatives listed on pages 49, this percentage could be reduced.

3. If you qualify for assistance through food stamps or have help from your church to meet food needs, this percentage could be reduced.

4. If you owe more than 5 percent of your net income or cannot make your budget balance, due to a heavy debt load, seek help from a Christian Financial Concepts volunteer counselor or Consumer Credit Counseling Service.

5. If you cannot allot 5 percent for Entertainment/Recreation because your budget is so tight, set aside *something* each month to take your children out to eat or on an outing. On page 60 you will find ideas for fun things you can do as a family that cost little or nothing.

6. Note: This percentage has not been factored into the total percentages shown for net income. In some cases, you may not have the money in your monthly income to adequately cover child care. See the alternatives for the Child Care category listed on page 63, including "125 Plan," or the Flexible Spending Account for dependent child care offered through your employer.

7. Considering the obligations at this income level, there may be no surplus for investing long term.

8. This category is used *only* when surplus income is received. This would be kept in the checking account to be used within a few weeks or transferred to an allocated category.

Chapter 6

BUDGET ANALYSIS

After you have recorded your present spending level and reviewed the percentage guidelines, you are ready to take the next step in establishing a new workable budget. Keep in mind that for your budget to work, your total expenses must not exceed your Net Spendable Income. Your job will be to decide which areas can be reduced to limit overspending or adjusted to work within the limits of an income that is too small.

STEP ONE: COMPARE

Look at what you are spending now (Existing Budget) compared to what you should be spending. The following steps will guide you in your analysis. If you need further assistance in figuring your budget, you can ask someone to help you. Or you can write to Christian Financial Concepts and request assistance from a qualified referral counselor near you.

- If you have not done so, copy Form 3 (Appendix), Budget Percentage Guidelines, and figure dollar amounts for each category.
- Copy the Budget Analysis sheet, Form 4 in the Appendix.
- Write the dollar amounts you came up with for each category in the monthly guideline budget column.
- Write the amounts you're currently spending in the existing budget column.
- Compare the two columns and enter the difference with a plus or minus in the difference column.

Note: A negative figure indicates a deficit; a positive number indicates a surplus.

STEP TWO: ANALYZE

After comparing the *Existing* and *Guideline* columns, you are ready to take the next step: develop a budget that reflects changes that need to be made. A new budget will help you to control spending in certain areas, or at least reduce them, to live within the *means* (your income) God has provided for you. That's why we've included many ideas in the following pages on reducing expenses in the budget categories.

It is not necessary that your new budget fit the guideline budget. What is important is that *your new budget does not exceed your Net Spendable Income.* If you haven't already, at this point it may be necessary to get some financial counseling to help you analyze your budget and make wise decisions.

STEP THREE: DECIDE

Once the total picture is reviewed, it is necessary to decide where the adjustments must be made and the spending reduced. It may be necessary to consider a change in housing, automobile, insurance, schooling, or some other category. The creative alternatives and money-saving strategies in the next chapter may help in those decisions.

Remember, *the minimum objective* of any budget should be to meet your family's needs without creating any further debt.

CONSIDERATIONS FOR VARIABLE INCOME

One of the most difficult problems in budgeting is allocating monthly spending when your income fluctuates. The normal tendency is to spend the money when it comes in or to treat higher months' income as windfall profits, which usually causes havoc in lower-income months.

Some suggestions for living on a fluctuating income:

1. Base your budget on an average of several low-income months.
2. Add 5 percent to your variable expenses from last year.
3. If you are beginning your budget during a lower-income month, delay funding some variable expenses until funds are available.
4. Keep business and personal expenses separate.
5. Use a separate checking account for business.
6. As funds come in, deposit them in a special savings account and draw a salary each month.

If you are paid every two weeks, rather than twice monthly, you will have two extra paychecks a year. Use these paychecks to fund some of the non-monthly expenses, such as car repairs, vacations, or clothing. The same applies for tax refunds, bonuses, and gifts.

Chapter 7

STRATEGIES FOR MAKING ENDS MEET

Once you have reviewed your total financial picture in the Budget Analysis, you can begin to decide where to make changes so spending can be reduced. Review the following alternatives, creative options, and suggestions for adjustments in the budget categories and decide which ones will work best for you.

Make another copy of Form 1 from the Appendix to create your new budget.

CATEGORY 1: TAXES

- Include all taxes you pay in the taxes category, even if you receive a refund.
- If taxes are paid once a year, divide amount by 12 for a monthly amount.
- If self-employment taxes are paid quarterly, divide amount by 3 for monthly amount.

Note: Tax refunds are counted as income. Since refunds are paid annually, divide by 12 for a monthly amount.

EARNED INCOME CREDIT (EIC)

EIC is a tax incentive for low-income working families that reduces federal taxes to as low as zero percent, and some families receive refunds above what was paid in federal taxes. To apply for EIC:

- Pick up Schedule EIC forms at your local IRS or post office.
- If the workbook is not included, ask for one.
- If you have questions about the form, call the local IRS office.
- File form with your federal 1040, 1040 A, or 1040 EZ form.

Note: Check with the local Community Action Agency to see if they offer free tax services to low income families. Also, someone in your church may be able to help you fill out your forms.

Everybody must pay taxes, including single parents with small incomes. The amount of your tax liability will vary, based on your income and expenses. Federal, state, and local taxes must be deducted from gross income. And no one can escape the Social Security tax (FICA).

If you work for someone, these are deducted before you are paid. But if you are self-employed, don't forget to set aside money for quarterly prepayments on taxes. In my counseling, I have often encountered single parents who owed substantial amounts to the IRS because they failed to pay taxes on self-employed income.

There are many ways to reduce taxes. A good accountant or tax consultant can help you discover what deductions you may be able to subtract from your taxes. For example, if you are self-employed, check for deductions for child care, use of your car in your work, or expenses you pay to keep a home office. In addition, funds can be set aside for certain expenses **before** your taxes are deducted from your pay if your company offers a flexible spending plan or a retirement investment plan.

CATEGORY 2: TITHES

Since the term *tithe* means "a tenth," let's assume you give 10 percent of your total income to God. Proverbs 3:9-10 tells us to "honor" God from the best of our resources, and the apostle Paul wrote about the heart attitude that God blesses.

"Honor the Lord from your wealth, and from the first of all your produce; so your barns will be filled with plenty, and your vats will overflow with new wine. Let each one do just as he has purposed in his heart; not grudgingly or under compulsion; for God loves a cheerful giver" (Proverbs 3:9; 2 Corinthians 9:7).

GIVING TO GOD reminds us who He is, who we are, and what our relationship should be to the things He has allowed us to manage in His name. Giving must be done in love, with a thankful and willing heart—all the time recognizing that God is the owner of everything.

There is a spiritual principle at work. As one single mother of three children states, "My tithe is a considerable amount of money when there is so little to spare. But I have found when I tithe, somehow the bills get paid even when it seems impossible. But if I don't tithe, then the worries come. I find careless spending is more of a temptation. Then I get behind on the bills. And through it all, I have always had plenty to eat and clothes to wear."

CATEGORY 3: HOUSING EXPENSES

This percentage is going to vary tremendously, depending on your area of the country, your other expenses, and whether you are receiving housing assistance.

Housing includes either rent or mortgage payment and all monthly expenses neces-

sary to operate the home, including taxes, insurance, maintenance, utilities, and telephone. Total Housing expenses should not be more than 40 percent of your NSI (Net Spendable Income).

Check the following housing alternatives and options that could reduce your Housing costs.

- **Become an apartment manager** where your rent and all housing expenses are free in exchange for your management of the apartment complex.

- **Rent one or more bedrooms** in your home to another parent, an unmarried person, or college student. Remember, however, to avoid ungodly appearances by being sure the boarder is the same sex as you. Watch for any harmful behavior around your children.

- **Rent a room to an international student** attending a local college or university who wants to polish English skills. Check references and be sure there are no language barriers—so you can at least understand each other enough to communicate.

- **Subsidized housing** is scarce. Sometimes there is a waiting period just to apply, and once you have been approved, you may have to wait a long time before a unit is available. Check with your local housing authority for eligibility, availability, and location.

- **Look for a housing** *co-op*. A housing co-op is a condo or apartment community that is privately owned and regulated by the members who live there. Payments are based on income, so payments increase as your income increases, but each unit has an established limit to the maximum payment. There are usually long waiting lists to apply, so if you locate one you're interested in, sign up as soon as possible.

- **Habitat for Humanity.** If you are working and have a stable income but cannot buy a home, check into applying for a Habitat for Humanity home. By putting in "sweat equity," many single parents who could not purchase a home any other way have become home-owners. For details on requirements and the application process, call the Habitat for Humanity office near you.

- **Low-income single parent housing** is available in some communities through non-profit organizations, usually Christian. Most of the multi-unit facilities are specifically designed to meet the immediate needs of single mothers and their children for a limited time—usually twenty-four months. They usually require residents to have an educational goal or work training that can be completed within their stay. Budgets are established and rent is charged according to the budget. Some provide child care; others help mothers locate subsidized child care. Some accept mothers on welfare; others require mothers to work. Some are funded by government funds; others are funded by churches and donations. If you have no other resource for housing you can afford, check around your community to see if there is a single parent housing program available and what the requirements are.

- **Home ownership may be a good option**, if you plan to stay in a community for an extended time—five to seven years at least—and if your job is secure enough to take on a mortgage. You might consider a new home, a townhouse or condominium, a prebuilt or mobile home, or remodeling a fixer-upper. (See Appendix G for more information on purchasing a home.)

- **Learn simple home repairs and do them yourself.** You can go to a major home center store and take classes on almost everything. It's also good, if you can, to subscribe to a do-it-yourself magazine such as *Family Handyman*, or if you can't check your local library. This magazine has a monthly section called "How a House Works," which gives basic information about different systems in a home. Become familiar with power tools and purchase your own. For what you would have to pay a repair person, you could buy your own power tool for that repair, and the tool is yours to use next time!

LITTLE SAVINGS IN HOME UTILITIES ADD UP!

- Don't keep water running constantly when washing dishes or brushing teeth.

- If you use an automatic dishwasher, wipe dishes before loading, run only when full, and turn off the heavy soil and dryer settings, or wash dishes by hand and drip dry.

- Keep a clean container filled with water in the refrigerator for quick cold drinks (it could even be a clean milk carton).

- Keep refrigerator door closed, and to get in and out quickly, put a list of what's inside on the door.

- Turn refrigerator to the lowest possible setting that still keeps food cold or frozen.

- Turn your water heater down. Most are set high enough to scald skin.

- Take quick showers instead of baths.

- Turn your heater thermostat down a few degrees in cold weather. Wear sweaters, robes, or socks if you're cold. Turn it down a few degrees more if nobody is going to be home.

- If you must use air conditioning in your climate, keep your thermostat set on the highest setting that you can be comfortable. Turn it up just a little when nobody will be home—it costs more to cool a hot house than it does to maintain a cooler one.

- Train family members to turn lights out when leaving a room.

- Keep outside doors closed; invite visitors in or step outside to talk.

- Limit watching TV, playing video games, and using the computer, if you have them, and turn off unattended televisions and radios.

- Keep washer and dryer filters clean. Use the proper water level and temperature settings and wash full loads whenever possible. Don't use second rinse cycles; presoak instead.

- Other hints are often provided by local utility companies.

CATEGORY 4: FOOD EXPENSES

The part of your Net Spendable Income you spend for food should not be more than 15 percent. The total amount you spend on food should be put in the Food category, plus, if you are receiving government food stamps, the amount you receive every month should be added to your Income category under "Other."

If you do not know your actual food expenses, keep a detailed spending record for thirty to forty-five days: include all grocery expenses, including paper goods and non-food (pet food, cleaning supplies) products purchased at grocery stores. Eating out is not included here because it falls under Entertainment expenses, not food expenses.

After doing all you can to stretch your food dollars, you may still have difficulty keeping up with your family's food needs. Your local church may be a good resource if they offer a food pantry for people in need.

If your church doesn't have a food pantry, they may refer you to another food pantry, or provide emergency funds or gift certificates from area stores for you to buy what you need.

Some Ways to Reduce Food Costs and Stretch Your Food Allocation

- Avoid buying junk foods (soft drinks, pretzels, chips, cookies). Instead, prepare your own treats.
- Buy breads, hamburger buns, rolls, and bagels at the bakery outlets for much less.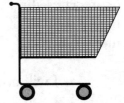
- Buy the store specials and bargains advertised in store flyers or in the food section of the newspaper—usually Wednesday or Thursday.
- Buy house brands and generic products whenever possible.
- Buy roasts and chicken in larger portions and repackage in zip-lock freezer bags or aluminum foil to freeze and use later. They usually are less expensive per pound in larger quantities.
- Always check the "sell by" and "use by" dates on products, especially dairy or meat products.
- Avoid buying convenience foods, such as grated cheese, prepackaged salads, or shredded vegetables.
- Avoid buying prepared foods, such as frozen dinners and microwave-ready meals. Instead, cook in quantity and freeze to have meals for several weeks ahead.
- Buy in bulk if you have a place to store large amounts and if you can use all of a product while it is good. Splitting a bulk purchase is even better, if you can find someone to divide with.
- Clip and use coupons when the products are ones you buy anyway but only when the price of the item with the coupon is less than a good store brand. Be sure to compare prices. To get extra savings, redeem the coupons on "double coupon" days.
- A little more spent on healthy choices—fresh vegetables, fruits, and grains—will

save on doctor bills and time off from work to care for sick children.

- Always shop with a list, and avoid grocery shopping when you are tired or hungry. For additional savings, plan your menus ahead—before you make your list.

- If you shop at a warehouse or club, *know your prices* and *stick to your list*. Although you can save money on some products and by buying bulk, warehouse shopping isn't always cheaper.

- Decrease paper product use by using cloth napkins and cloth towels in the kitchen; using newspaper to clean windows (if you don't take the paper perhaps a neighbor would save some for you); and peeling vegetables onto newspaper or onto plastic bags you brought your groceries home in.

- Watch store flyers for sales and rebates on frequently used items like shampoo, deodorant, bar soap, and detergent.

CATEGORY 5: AUTOMOBILE EXPENSES

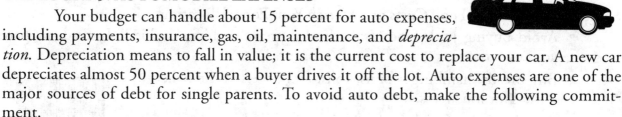

Your budget can handle about 15 percent for auto expenses, including payments, insurance, gas, oil, maintenance, and *depreciation*. Depreciation means to fall in value; it is the current cost to replace your car. A new car depreciates almost 50 percent when a buyer drives it off the lot. Auto expenses are one of the major sources of debt for single parents. To avoid auto debt, make the following commitment.

- I will not buy a car I can't afford.
- I will not use credit cards to buffer my car repair expenses.

_____
(Signed)

The Automobile category is one in which you will need to be extremely disciplined and trust God for what you cannot provide for yourself.

That's because, without some intervention from outside their own budget, many single parents do not have the income to replace their worn-out cars.

The cheapest car you'll ever drive is the one you own, but it will need maintenance to keep it running properly.

Some Cost-Cutting Ideas for Auto Maintenance

- Many vocational and technical colleges have auto-mechanic departments and do routine maintenance, tune-ups, and/or repairs on cars for little or no cost (but be sure eager auto students are supervised by a qualified teacher).

- Find a family member or friend who is knowledgeable about auto maintenance to help you with routine checks, oil changes, tire and brake checks, and the like.

- If your car needs repairs, find a professional mechanic in your circle of friends or relatives who wants to make some money on the side in a home garage; this way you may only have to pay for the parts.

- Learn all you can about auto maintenance. You can do some of the maintenance yourself, with some tips from a knowledgeable friend. Be sure you know what you are doing, and it is wise to have a professional check your work.

- A car care ministry, or a car maintenance co-op, is an excellent service for churches to provide. A typical car ministry involves a group of Christians who meet regularly, perhaps once a month on Saturdays at a church parking lot, to perform routine maintenance and minor car repairs on the cars of single parents or widows. If your church doesn't have a car care ministry, suggest that they contact Christian Financial Concepts for guidelines on getting such a ministry started.

WAYS TO CUT CAR EXPENSES

Save money on car insurance. If your car is more than five years old and you have completely paid for it, carry only liability insurance (required by law). If you owe on your car, your bank will require full coverage.

Shop and compare prices on liability insurance.

Save money on tires. Go to a tire dealer and ask for "take-offs"—tires that have been taken off a new car because the buyer wanted a different kind. Take-offs are nearly new and often half the price of brand new tires.

Do preventative maintenance on your car. Check the library for books on car ownership that offer money-saving and maintenance tips or sign up for a class. About every 25,000 to 30,000 miles the average car needs tires, brakes, belts, and spark plugs. Even if it is difficult to afford routine maintenance, it can save you from bigger problems later on. Your car will be safer, have fewer breakdowns, use less fuel, and have a higher resale value.

BUYING A CAR

You should buy a newer car if:

1. You have to drive extra-long distances.
2. You have to use your car for your job/travel.
3. Your present car is worn out.

Remember, about 15 percent of your Net Spendable Income should be allotted for Automobile expenses. Since buying a mid-range new car commonly runs in excess of $400 a month (including payments, insurance, maintenance), look for a good used car or a demo or "program" car.

Action Point

Write your current automobile needs, including repairs and replacement if the car is worn out:

Determine how much you will spend on replacing your car, and do not waiver on the amount:

_____

Write the options you can be flexible with to get a better deal:

_____

_____

If you're spending too much on auto expenses or can't afford repairs or replacement of your car, how will you handle meeting those needs:

_____

_____

_____

_____

If you simply cannot afford to replace a car that can no longer be repaired, you need to pray and trust God for the answer. One single mother whose income was so low she could not replace her car received four different cars from four different sources over a five year period. The cars were older models on their "last legs," but they lasted until another came. In between cars, friends helped her get back and forth to work.

Automobile Insurance

Depending on where you live, *liability insurance* may be required by law. Liability insurance covers injuries to occupants and damages to any car you hit with your car, if the accident is your fault. However, if you have an automobile loan through a bank, you also are required to carry *comprehensive coverage*, which covers theft and damage to your car caused by fire, vandalism, hail, or something other than a collision; *collision coverage* provides coverage in case your car collides with another object or turns over. Complete coverage also can include uninsured motorist insurance, towing and emergency service, car rental coverage, or loaner cars if yours is being repaired due to an accident.

Work with your financial counselor and a trustworthy insurance agent in your church to determine what your car insurance needs are. Also, review the suggestions below; they offer ways to reduce your auto insurance costs.

Ways to Lower Your Auto Insurance Costs
- **Comparison shop.** Ask for recommendations from friends, check consumer guides.
- **Use a higher deductible**, if you can keep enough in savings to cover it.
- **Drop collision and/or comprehensive coverage** if your car is worth less than $1,000 and paid for.

- **Ask about discounts.** Different companies offer discounts for low mileage drivers, automatic seat belts, anti-lock brakes, air bags, good driving records, good grades for students, driver training courses, non-drinking drivers, and so on.
- **Buy a low-profile car.** Check insurance costs before you buy. Avoid thieves' favorites.

CATEGORY 6: INSURANCE

This category includes all insurance, such as health, life, and disability—anything not associated with the home or auto. Guidelines for figuring insurance needs, types of insurance, and other related topics, such as will, trusts, Social Security, and veteran's benefits, are covered in a free pamphlet called "Everything a Widow Needs to Know" which covers these topics in more detail. Call CFC's materials line, 1-800-722-1976, to receive a copy, or download a copy from CFC's Internet pages (http://www.cfcministry.org). This resource is not only beneficial for widows but for anyone who works with widows, married couples who are planning ahead, and other single parents who are considering marriage. Being prepared, knowing resources, and having support can save a new widow tremendous anguish during a very difficult period.

Life Insurance

When funds are limited, life insurance should be a lower priority than health coverage. The fact is, some single parents really don't need life insurance. Life insurance should be used only to provide—never to profit or protect. The Lord should be our protection, and profiting should be a strategy of an investment plan, not an insurance plan. Therefore, if you have children that are grown and on their own, minor children that could be cared for by other family members, or investments or retirement funds that could be used to provide for your children if you died, you may not need life insurance.

However, if you still have minor to college-age children, you will need life insurance if there are no other resources to provide for them. If your income is low, and you can free only a small amount per month, buy the least expensive coverage you can with the available dollars. Annual renewable term life insurance provides the greatest death benefit for the least cost. It accumulates no cash value but, remember, provision is the primary concern, not profit.

Insurance Coverage on Children

Some people are concerned about covering burial expenses in case a child dies. This is understandable, but insurance may not be the solution. If your child's other parent is still living and available, check to see if his or her insurance through work covers the death of a minor child. If no coverage is provided, then ask the Memorial Society about a family membership.

You probably have seen some low-cost insurance plans that usually are offered specifically for children. Premium payments are low when children are small and increase as they age. However, rather than spending money on these plans, savings or investments are a better way to cover these expenses in the long run.

Disability Insurance

Disability insurance provides income for people who are declared legally to be no longer able to work in their occupation because of an accident or illness. The majority of people are not going to become permanently disabled. Extra insurance to cover disability is generally too expensive for most single parents to even consider and is only worth considering if you have additional funds to spend. In the event that you do become totally disabled, Social Security will provide income benefits if you have worked at least five years for employers that deducted Social Security from your pay.

If you become disabled from an accident or exposure to something toxic at work, you may qualify for worker's compensation or disability through the company, if they are proven to be responsible for your injuries or illness. When a disability claim is filed, usually you don't receive any income while the claim is being processed but, once the claim is approved, the income and benefits will be retroactive to the application date. This means that your coverage will begin at the time you applied, not when you were approved, so all the money you were entitled to from the date you applied would be paid.

Burial Coverage

The Memorial Society, a non-profit organization, helps members lower the cost of burial expenses. The Society:

- Is available in most states.
- Requires a small one-time fee to join; some states require a small annual fee.
- Offers individual and family memberships.

The Memorial Society's phone number is 800-765-0107.

Health Insurance

Most companies provide a company-sponsored group health insurance plan and require employees to pay part of the expense for these plans, but they offer several options to help keep the costs low for the employees. If your children are covered under your health plan or their other parent's health plan, find out what benefits are available, how to process a claim, and how much of the uncovered expenses and deductibles you will have to pay.

Medicaid

Some churches and counselors recommend that single parents apply to welfare for Medicaid benefits when no other options seem to be available. However, I don't believe people, especially Christians, should have to go to the government to meet their needs. God's Word instructs families to care for their own first. If the family cannot help, then there are other alternatives available.

Alternative Health Care

Some Christian organizations offer health plans similar to insurance, except that the members share their particular medical situation and the expense is met by the other members. Costs and services vary, so be sure you thoroughly investigate the plan you're interested in for benefits, deductibles, and exclusions. Also, as with any business you're not familiar with, check for any complaints registered with the Better Business Bureau, or a similar organization in your community.

The following is provided for you to begin your own research into alternative health plans:

- Christian Brotherhood 800-269-4030
- All Saints 800-259-0095
- Good Samaritan 317-861-1424

Many single parents who have needed support from the church found it lacking. If you've gone to your church and received a poor response, you have some options. If your church wants to help but is not prepared to, you can be instrumental in helping start a ministry that cares for the needs of single parents.

The least the church can do is to let the membership know of the need, help meet emergency expenses, and build a resource list of doctors, dentists, and other medical facilities that will treat low income patients for fees, based on what they can afford to pay. If your church doesn't see the need for this type of ministry, consider looking for another church that is interested before applying for government funds.

If you are already receiving government help or there is no other option for you but to apply for government funds, go ahead and use the benefits, but promise yourself you will not take advantage of the benefits any longer than you have to.

CATEGORY 7: DEBT

Copy the list of Debts sheet, Form 8 from the Appendix. List all debts, including non-monthly debts such as doctor bills, family loans, bank notes, repairs, and other occasional expenses. Include the address and phone number of each creditor for a quick reference if you have a problem with payments.

> The simplest economic principle ever written: If you don't borrow money, you can't get into debt.

It is recommended that you spend no more than 5 percent of your NSI on all debt payments. If you've been subsidizing your income to creditors, you will find it very difficult to balance your budget. However, here are some potential solutions.

1. Contact creditors with a plan for how much you can pay them.

2. Never promise creditors more than you can realistically pay.

3. Pay the smallest debt first, then add the amount you were paying to the next debt, and so on until all the debts are paid.

4. Obtain the help of a financial counselor through CFC or Consumer Credit Counseling to make arrangements with creditors.

5. Stick with your agreements. You will be dropped from Consumer Credit Counseling if you don't, and will be hounded again by creditors.

6. File for bankruptcy under Chapter 13 of the Federal Bankruptcy Act. This provides court protection while debts are being paid.

7. Reestablish a clean credit record.

"It is better that you should not vow than that you should vow and not pay" (Ecclesiastes 5:5).

"The wicked borrows and does not pay back, but the righteous is gracious and gives" (Psalms 37:21).

HOW GOD PROVIDED

I have been a single parent now for three years and learned some valuable financial lessons. I sought God's will for our lives and was anxious to obey what I found in Scripture. With a cheerful heart, I tithed a portion of my settlement to a church that had come alongside us in the depths of our troubles, as we trusted and waited for God's will in our lives. The prayers of these saints upheld us through a very difficult time.

Within the month, an entry level position opened at this same church and three people called [to] encourage me to apply for the job. One week later, I found myself in the position and my child in the church's excellent child care program at a reduced cost. God was gracious to both of us.

However, after the first six months and accumulating $2,600 in debt, I realized that my paycheck was not covering our expenses. Wandering the halls, I began to pray about this situation, asking God who could help us. The one person that kept coming to mind was the business manager of the church . . . I was too embarrassed to confess such an error.

Finally I called and set up a meeting with him. We went through the painful task of putting my financial obligations on paper. A friend joined us in the meeting and brought out Larry Burkett's book . . . [The Complete Financial Guide for Single Parents]. It was very painful to find out where my money was going and where it was supposed to be going. We discussed ways to bring the expenses in line with my income and then lifted the whole situation up to the Lord in prayer. It was not going to be easy and would not come overnight, but now I had a group of people to whom I was accountable and they were sincerely praying for our needs.

They also suggested I meet with Consumer Credit Corporation, where I turned in my credit cards and they called [my] creditors to stop interest [from] accruing and set up a plan for getting [me] out of debt. I made one payment a month which was distributed among the creditors. This month I will make the final payment and be debt-free!

God blessed my petitions and instead of criticism and rejection at our church, we received His "tender mercies" (Psalm 145:9). Bags of clothes for my daughter would appear in my office from time to time. I began attending a wonderful Bible study for women that is full of many gracious, mature believers. I needed financial help with car repairs and even an apartment deposit, and the Benevolence Committee was willing to help in these matters.

Where are we now? Since that time, God has continued to teach and guide my family as we rebuilt our lives. My daughter attends a day school at the church and I have been blessed with a change in positions within the church, increasing my earnings. With debt decreasing, I have been able to save a small portion from each paycheck, and above all—tithe. I have even had the privilege of sharing some of my own hard lessons and [sharing] Larry's book with other moms who are perplexed by the financial responsibilities they now face as single parents.

Truly, here is the body of Christ in faith and action. They did not pity us and send us on as James speaks of in James 2:15 but recognized and met our physical and spiritual needs. They are still standing by us as we are living God's will for our lives. "Religion that God our Father accepts as pure and faultless is this: to look after orphans and widows in their distress and to keep oneself from being polluted by the world" (James 1:27).

Paula Rupp, Youth and College Division
Highland Park Presbyterian Church
Dallas, Texas

In situations I've seen in which repayment of debts seemed impossible, once the individual made an absolute commitment to pay what was legitimately due, God provided the means to do so.

The book, *Debt-Free Living* (Moody Press) offers a more comprehensive look at becoming debt-free. It is available through CFC or your local Christian bookstore.

CATEGORY 8: ENTERTAINMENT/RECREATION

"The biggest discouragement for my children and me after the divorce was to think there were so many things we couldn't do as a family anymore that just weren't in the budget—like movies and vacations," said one single mom. Actually, she found they just had to find a different way of doing things for entertainment and recreation—rethinking recreation—but not doing without it completely. You need fun times together as a family.

Low cost suggestions for family fun:

- Summer musicals, symphonies, or dramas in the park. Take a picnic dinner.
- Library and mall events, such as puppet shows, craft demonstrations, or Logo events.
- Recreation department events, such as craft classes, square dancing, or sports.
- Holiday activities, such as making cookies or crafts for gifts, or Christmas caroling.
- Museums, festivals, and theaters; clip special offers for children from the newspaper.
- Movie night; check out movies, at no charge, at the local library. Pop popcorn.
- School book clubs; buy discount books and accumulate bonus points for free products.
- Summer camps; Christian camps are listed in denominational newsletters, local Christian newspapers, church bulletins, and national Christian magazines. For example, Focus on the Family offers a sports camp for boys from single parent homes (call 719-531-3400 for details). Other camps are listed in local newspapers, usually in the spring.

 *Bright Idea:*

On certain weekends, a single mom from Indiana offers to baby sit children from her church—so her son has someone to play with, the other parent gets a break, and she is able to get things done around the house without hearing how bored he is. Then when his friends leave, she is free to spend "Saturday special time" with him and go to the park or go fishing—their favorite hobby. She adds, "Fishing is an inexpensive hobby, and bowling is cheaper on Sunday afternoons!"

CATEGORY 9: CLOTHING EXPENSES

It is recommended that you spend no more than 5 percent of your Net Spendable Income for clothing. Figure the average annual amount spent on clothes and divide by twelve. The minimum amount should be at least $10 per month per family member. On a budget of $15,000 a year gross income, you should allocate about 5 percent of net income or about $50 per month for clothing.

Two things are apparent at first glance at this figure: First, most single parents usually don't have $50 a month in their budgets for clothing. Second, even if they did, $50 won't go very far today—for two or three people. Since clothing you and your family is a big challenge on a tight budget, you might follow these three principles.

1. Allocate at least something on a monthly basis for replacement of clothing.
2. Eliminate all use of credit cards to buy clothes you can't afford.
3. Allow God to provide some of your needs from other people's surplus.

Strategies for Stretching Your Clothing Dollar

- **Stage a clothing exchange.** Pick a theme, such as "children's clothes and shoes, for the season. A committee would need to sort clothes according to size, and give leftovers to charity.
- **Consignment shops and thrift stores.** You find good buys if you're alert shopper, and you can make money on your unwanted items. Call the shop for an appointment to drop clothing off.
- **Yard and garage sales.** For best selection, go early; they're an excellent source for kitchen appliances or children's educational toys and books. Have your own sale for extra money.
- **Care for clothing.** Mend holes and tears as soon as possible, use cold water to preserve colors.
- **Avoid "dry clean only" clothing.** Read labels carefully; some can be washed if care is taken.
- **Buy basic colors.** Coordinate your wardrobe around classic, traditional styles you can wear through several seasons.
- **Buy during sales.** Shop discount stores. Look for bargain racks with seasonal close outs.
- **Give children a clothing allowance.** Seasonally or annually, as soon as they are old enough.

CATEGORY 10: SAVINGS

Every family should save something—no matter the amount. The allocation for the savings category should be about 5 percent. A savings account can provide the following.

- Funds for emergencies
- Funds for needs that cannot be anticipated.
- Financial freedom as a result of good planning.

Unless savings are accumulated for unexpected expenses, the use of credit cards is a certainty.

One practical way to start saving is to put part of all additional income into your savings account. This includes cash gifts, overtime income, bonuses, garage sale profits, and the like. Once you make a commitment to becoming totally debt-free, God can bless you in many ways. But if you never make the commitment, the additional money most likely will be spent. There always seems to be inexhaustible needs in your life as a single parent. Even so, savings must become an absolute priority.

CATEGORY 11: MEDICAL/DENTAL

Medical Expenses include insurance deductibles, doctor and dental bills, eyeglasses, prescription drugs, and orthodontist visits and should be at least 5 percent of your NSI. Use a yearly average divided by twelve to determine a monthly amount.

Since this is an area that causes havoc in most single parents' budgets, here are some ways to deal with medical expenses.

- **Share your need.** Let other Christians know if you can't meet expenses.
- **Tell the doctor your situation** before you run up medical bills. Some are willing to provide low-cost service to low-income clients.
- **Barter for services.** Offer to clean the office, baby-sit, do yard work, and so on, to cut costs.
- **Take advantage of dental schools** for cleaning, fillings, or other treatments. Costs are about half of what private dentists or orthodontists charge, and students are supervised.

CATEGORY 12: MISCELLANEOUS

This category covers just about everything else not included in other categories. Several suggestions on how to save money in this category have already been given, but more can be said since this category includes what many single parents consider "options." Although a lot can be cut from this category, be sure you don't cut what you really need.

Savings Suggestions

- **Discount stores, discount pharmacies, or closeout stores** usually offer brand name or generic equivalents at lower prices.
- **Beauty and barber colleges** provide low-cost perms, hair-coloring, and cuts. Barter with a friend who is a licensed stylist, or color your hair yourself.
- **School lunch program.** To see if your family is eligible, check with the school.
- **Cut subscriptions** to magazines and mail order services.

 *Bright Idea:*

One single parent said, "My kids have allergies, so we have to buy a particular brand of soap and there's no generic available. The soap is more expensive than other soaps, but buying the soap costs less than dermatology treatments. I found a store that discounts the soap twice a year. They sell six bars for the price of three and have a limit of two packages per customer. I buy two boxes each time I visit the store during the sale, and that keeps me supplied practically all year for about half the regular price."

CATEGORY 13: CHILD CARE

The single parent Budget Guideline allows for no more than 15 percent of your income for Child Care. In fact, if you add the percentages of all the other categories together, you will notice that 100 percent of your income will be designated before you get to this category. ***Therefore, all other categories must be reduced to provide these funds.*** This expense differs so dramatically from one single parent family to another that each situation must be handled individually.

About 40 percent of all single parents have the extra financial burden of paying for some type of child care. The other 60 percent either have families who help or older children who can baby-sit; or, they work at home, stay at home, or do not work a steady job. In some parts of the country, like Washington, D.C., good full-time child care can cost up to $150 a week. There is no magic formula to making child care expenses fit into your budget, but here are some other ideas that may help.

Child Care Suggestions
- **Church-based programs.** Some offer sliding scale fees to low-income families.
- **Pre-K programs.** In some states, pre-K programs for 4 to 5-year-olds are funded by the state. Only after school care would need to be provided.
- **Head Start.** The government-based program provides preschool for ages 3 to 5. Christian parents should check program curriculum carefully.
- **In-home providers** usually charge much less than centers, and provide a better ratio of care.
- **Start a day care business** in your home. Check for local requirements and regulations. Benefits include ministry opportunities with other children, tax deductions for home businesses, and a safe environment for your children. Keep good records, save receipts, and consult with a tax advisor.
- **Keep your children home** by starting a home-based business. See Chapter 10 for ways to make money at home.
- **Swap baby-sitting** with a friend that has a different schedule.
- **Private schools.** This can be affordable, even for the single parent, if the school offers a scholarship program. Parents may be able to exchange services to help pay tuition.

 *Bright Idea*

When B.J. was left to provide for her child, she was a paralegal; yet she wanted to be home with her son. When she was laid off from her job, she rented out a room to help pay mortgage. She began doing day care part-time, nights and weekends, to make ends meet. Even when she got another paralegal job, she continued doing day care and was registered as a certified day care home. Soon after, she was able to quit and do full-time day care. B.J. actually did better financially with home day care as her primary source of income, had no child care expenses for her son, and has supported herself and her son the last five years. She was even able to manage without having to rent a room.

Paying Child Support

If you have been ordered to pay child support to care for your minor children, the monthly amount you pay should be included in the "Other" category under Child Care. As mentioned earlier, this should be a priority for parents. Children not only need both fathers and mothers to provide materially, they also need them to provide physically, emotionally, and spiritually. Even noncustodial parents can still parent effectively when they meet these needs. If you struggle with paying child support, remember, you can't expect God to bless you financially or honor your gifts to Him if you forsake your own children. Make the commitment to provide not only what is required by the court but also what is needed. God will honor your commitment. To decide whether you should invest, consider the following.

- Invested funds grow much faster than funds placed in insurance policies.
- Companies often contribute toward employees' investments in company sponsored plans.
- Costs can start low, especially if you find other investors to share in purchasing.

The Results

To figure your *Total Expenses*, add all the expenses you have planned for each category. Then deduct this amount from your Net Spendable Income. If you have money left over, place the amount on the line for Category 15: *Unallocated Surplus Income*. However, if you came up with a minus figure, you will need to make further changes to balance your budget.

CATEGORY 14: UNALLOCATED SURPLUS INCOME

You may find that sometimes you will have extra money available above what you had budgeted. You can simply transfer it to your savings account if the money is to be used later on. But if the money is going to be used within a few weeks, leave it in the checking account. This category was created just to hold these funds. This allows you to keep the other categories constant each month. It also serves as a good record of income for tax purposes.

Chapter 8

THE CONTROL SYSTEM

A budget that isn't used is a waste of time and effort. The most common reason a budget is discarded is because it's too complicated.

Envelope Budgeting System

You can start with the most basic budgeting system—the envelope system—unless you have experience managing the family finances.

- Divide available money into various envelopes for each category (Housing, Food, Auto).
- Withdraw money from appropriate envelope when needed or payment is due.
- Money orders are usually used to mail payments.
- Remember, no more spending for a category if the envelope is empty.
- If you borrow money from other envelopes, you'll have to determine how the other expenses will be paid.

With this system, you can readily see if funds are available when you need them. CFC has a low-cost envelope system called *The Cash Organizer* than can help you get organized.

Spending Control Plan

As soon as you are experienced and confident with your envelope budgeting system, you can move to the Spending Control Plan. The account control pages have been substituted for envelopes.

Using this budget system, all the money is deposited into a checking account and account control pages are used to accomplish what the envelopes once accomplished. How much is put into each account (or envelope) from monies received during the month is determined from the Income Allocation Sheet.

To find out what works for you, adapt the Spending Control Plan to your family's needs. This guide will help you to personalize your budget after you've developed the self-discipline to stay on the envelope plan or any other simple budget for six months.

For example, you may not have money for all twelve basic categories to start with. Instead of being overwhelmed at the forms and categories, just *start at the point that fits your needs*, but start somewhere. If you need help interpreting the forms or how to use the Individual Account pages or Checkbook Ledger, seek the help of a financial counselor or CPA in your church.

PLANNING - KEEPING TRACK - CONTROLLING

The system described in this workbook is the simplest, yet most complete, way possible to budget your money.

Keep It Simple

The Goal—Your goal is to decide the most you can spend in each category and to know where you are in regard to how much you have already spent at all times. Having excess money in a category does not indicate an opportunity to spend.

To know how much *should* be spent, how much *is* being spent, and how much is *left* to spend in each budget category, Individual Account pages have been substituted for envelopes. All the money is deposited into one checking account and these account pages accomplish what the envelopes once accomplished. The amount of money reserved for each account category is determined by your Income Allocation Sheet. (See figure below.)

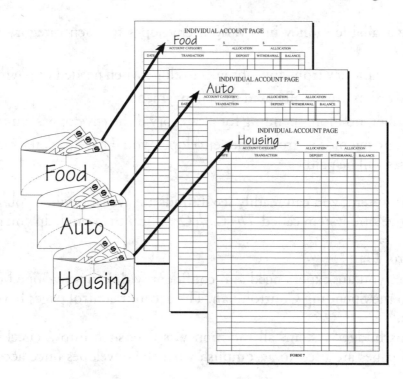

USE OF THE INCOME ALLOCATION PAGE (Form 5, Appendix)

The purpose of the Income Allocation sheet is to divide Net Spendable Income among the various budget categories. It is simply a plan to determine how each paycheck or income source is going to be spent.

Once you have determined from the budget analysis what you can reasonably spend for each category per month, write the amount in the Monthly Allocation column on a copy of Form 5.

Next, divide the monthly allocation for each category, such as Housing or Food, by pay period. See the following example. If the house payment is due by the end of the month, and the income is received twice a month, the allocation for Housing needs to be divided so that part of the money is reserved from each pay and all of it will be available when the payment is due. Utilities and other housing costs must be allocated the same way.

INCOME ALLOCATION

INCOME		INCOME SOURCE/PAY PERIOD			
		1st	2nd		
BUDGET CATEGORY	MONTHLY ALLOCATION	$1041	$1041		
1. Tithe	$208	$104	$104		
2. Tax	365	182.50	182.50		
3. Housing	573	423	150		
4. Food	200	100	100		
5. Auto	260	160	100		
6. Insurance	39	14	25		
7. Debts	90				

It is not necessary for your pay to be evenly divided. The important thing is that when a payment is due, the money is available. Therefore, some funds from middle-of-the-month pay periods must be held to meet obligations that come due at the first of the month. Failure to do this is a common source of budget problems.

You can use your current Income Allocation form until changes occur, such as paying off debts, a pay raise, or expenses change; then the form will need to be updated.

USE OF THE INDIVIDUAL ACCOUNT PAGES (Form 7, Appendix)

A separate account page should be used for each budget category, just as each category had its own envelope. Make enough copies of Form 7 to have one for each of the categories you have money allocated. At the top of each page, place the proper category title, such as Housing, Food, or Auto. Then place the amount that was allocated (on your Income Allocation form) from each pay period for that category in the blank allocation lines ($_____) at the top of the page. If you are paid more frequently than twice a month, add more allocation lines ($_____). This will help you remember how much is reserved from each pay period.

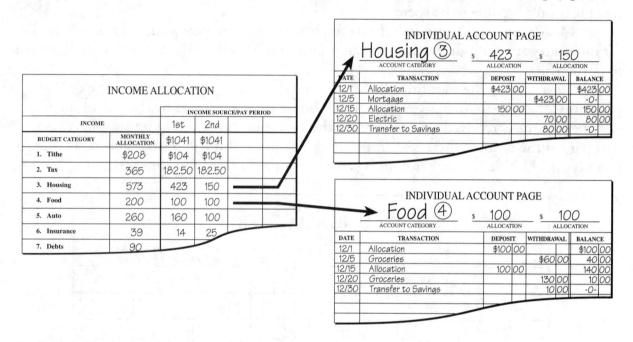

The purpose of the account page is to record *all transactions* (income and spending) in each category for the month. The allocation taken from each payday for the category is shown as a deposit, and each time money is spent, it is shown as a withdrawal.

The account page for each category should show a zero balance at the end of the month. If funds are left at the end of the month, transfer the money to your savings account to make your account page balance zero. If you run short of funds in a category, you may need to transfer money from savings to provide the needed funds (see example below). If a category is out of money when expenses are due, and savings are not available, you will have to decide how you will provide the funds.

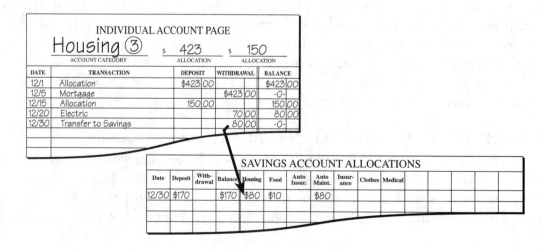

How to Use the Budget System

A good budget system should be kept as simple as possible, while accomplishing its goal: *To show if you spend more than you allocated each month.* Remember that this system is similar to using envelopes. If a specific amount of money is placed in the envelopes each month, you will know at a glance whether your budget balances. Obviously, with some non-monthly expenses to be budgeted, the system has to be a little more complicated. But don't overcomplicate it.

To help you better understand how to use the budget system, we'll take one category (Housing) through a typical month's transactions.

INCOME ALLOCATION

INCOME		INCOME SOURCE/PAY PERIOD			
		1st	2nd		
BUDGET CATEGORY	MONTHLY ALLOCATION	$1041	$1041		
1. Tithe	$208	$104	$104		
2. Tax	365	182.50	182.50		
3. Housing	573	423	150		
4. Food	200	100	100		
5. Auto	260	160	100		
6. Insurance	39	14	25		
7. Debts	90				

FORM 5

INDIVIDUAL ACCOUNT PAGE

Housing ③ $ 423 $ 150

DATE	TRANSACTION	DEPOSIT	WITHDRAWAL	BALANCE
12/1	Allocation	$423 00		$423 00
12/5	Mortgage		$423 00	-0-
12/15	Allocation	150 00		150 00
12/20	Electric		70 00	80 00
12/30	Transfer to Savings		80 00	-0-

FORM 7

The above illustration shows a budget in which the gross income of $2,083 per month is received in two pay periods of $1,041 each.

Pay Allocation—The two checks have been divided as evenly as possible among the necessary categories. For example, the tithe is paid each pay period (remember, it is based on gross income). The Housing allocation of $573 is divided, $423 in the first pay period, $150 in the second.

Housing Allocation—On the first pay period, a deposit of $423 is noted on the Account Page. On the second pay period, the mortgage is paid and noted as a withdrawal, leaving a balance of zero ($0).

Each transaction is noted similarly until, at the end of the month, a balance of $80 is left. This balance, or surplus, is then transferred to savings. The account starts at zero again next month.

Many people prefer to leave the surplus funds from each category in their checking account rather than transfer them to a savings account. This is fine, provided you can discipline yourself not to spend the money just because it's easily accessible. For some people, the total cash reserves in checking are enough to qualify for free checking privileges, which more than offset any loss of interest in a savings account.

Use of the Checkbook Ledger

To simplify your bookkeeping, I recommend using the Checkbook Ledger (Form 7a). If this seems too complicated, at least be sure all checkbook information is transferred immediately to the appropriate account pages, and indicate check numbers as a reference until you are accustomed to budgeting. After a little practice, time spent on budgeting will decrease. Then you can add another step.

Note that the Checkbook Ledger is just a slightly modified Form 7. Each deposit and withdrawal is recorded, and the resulting balance is shown. At the end of each month the ledger is *balanced* against the bank statement. If you use a checkbook that gives you a duplicate copy of each written check, you will be able to see if you have written any checks you forgot to record.

As you go through your bank statement, make a check mark by each entry you have verified. The ending balance on your checkbook statement will probably not match what you have in your checkbook ledger because you will have written checks that have not cleared the bank before your statement was sent. To balance your ledger with your statement, add the checks, withdrawals, and deposits that are listed on your checkbook ledger, but are not listed on your bank statement, to your ending bank balance. The resulting figure should match the current balance in your checkbook ledger.

Also note that the total balance in the example checkbook ledger matches the balance on the individual account sheets. The checkbook ledger balance should reflect all the balances from all the categories added together. Although the funds show zero in the example, because additional funds were transferred to savings, you still may have a balance because of money reserved in checking for expenses at the first of the next month.

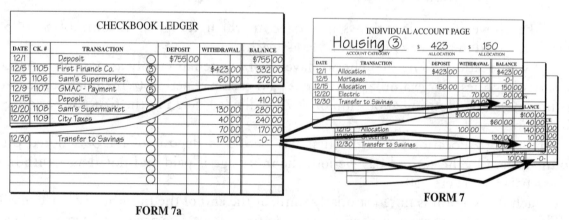

FORM 7a

FORM 7

If there are additional deposits or withdrawals from the bank statement recorded in the Checkbook Ledger, these must also be recorded on the appropriate budget Account Sheet. For example, a service charge from the bank would be listed as an expense in the Checkbook Ledger and as a Miscellaneous expense in category 12 of the budget.

The numbers shown in the circles (0) on Form 7a indicate which category account each check should be deducted from. It's common for most people to write a check and record, or *post*, the amount in the ledger, then record the amount on the Account Page later. To be sure that all checks are recorded on the proper Account Page, the category number should be entered only in the Checkbook Ledger after the check has been recorded on the proper Account Page.

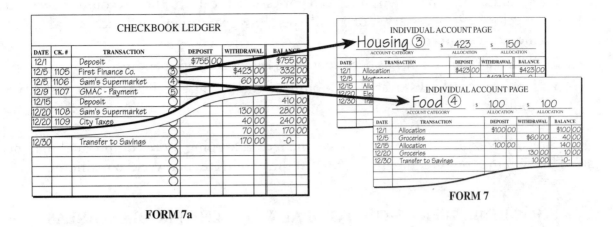

FORM 7a

FORM 7

Checking Account Notation

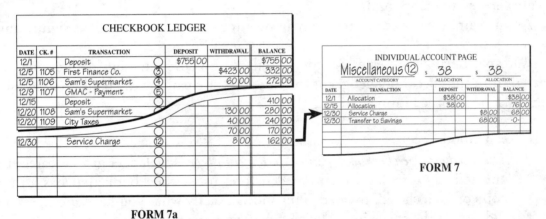

FORM 7a

FORM 7

Keep in mind that the goal of the system is to establish a level of spending for each category and to know where you are with respect to that level. The Account Pages (or envelopes) keep track of money in the check account. The savings allocation page keeps track of money in the savings account. Remember that the plan is to know what each dollar in the checking account is for and what each dollar in the savings account is for. When you spend money, you need to know which money is spent on clothes, food, auto, and so on.

Discipline

In order to provide the necessary control, you must discipline yourself to spend money based on the amount in the account (envelope) and not the amount in the checkbook.

Potential Problem Areas

Cash Withdrawals—Many times various expenses for the car (gas, repairs, and the like) are paid with personal cash. When using a budget, it is important to develop some rules for self-discipline, such as the following.

1. Separate personal cash into categories identical to the Account Pages. Use envelopes, if necessary, but avoid spending gas money for lunches and grocery money for entertainment.

2. When all the money has been spent in a category, stop spending.

3. Don't write checks over the amount of the actual purchases to get cash. Write another check and note it as "cash, personal."

Category Mixing—Don't try to make the record keeping more complicated than necessary. This system should require no more than thirty minutes per week to maintain.

BUDGET BUSTERS: HOW TO DEAL WITH THE PROBLEM AREAS

Bookkeeping Errors

An accurately balanced checkbook is a must. Even small errors result in big problems if they are allowed to compound.

An inaccurate balance can result in an overdrawn account, as well as significant bank charges.

Automatic banking creates another pitfall. Automatic payment deductions must be subtracted from the checkbook ledger at the time they are paid by the bank. ATM cash withdrawals must be recorded immediately.

How To Keep Good Records

1. *Use a ledger type checkbook rather than a stub type.* The ledger gives greater visibility and reduces errors. As mentioned before, use a checkbook that has a duplicate copy of each check provided. This shows exactly what you have spent, even if you didn't post the check in the ledger when you wrote it.

2. *Be sure all checks are accounted for.* All checks should be entered in your checkbook ledger when written. This entry must include the check number, amount, date, and the name of the person or store to whom you wrote the check. *Write all checks from the checkbook only,* and avoid tearing checks out of your checkbook for future use.

3. *Maintain a checkbook ledger at home.* If all records are kept just in your checkbook, you run the risk of losing your only written record. A home checkbook ledger eliminates this possibility and makes record keeping more orderly. Although you can obtain an up-to-date record from your bank, the record will not show the checks you wrote that have not yet cleared the bank.

   As mentioned earlier, it is recommended that separate checks be written for each category. If you buy motor oil or magazines at the grocery store and write one check to cover these items and the groceries, you will have mixed categories. A separate checkbook ledger at home provides space to break down expenses, if needed.

Chapter 9

MAKING INCOME THROUGH A HOME BUSINESS

About 10 percent of the U.S. population, or over 28 million people, now work at least part time in their home. Some of these home workers are professionals, who with the availability of home computers, fax machines, and modems can work out of home offices. Others are working part-time to supplement their incomes with small businesses.

A stay-at-home job that brings in even a couple hundred dollars a month often can make the difference for a single parent who is struggling to make ends meet. With the savings in child care, transportation, fast food, and work clothing, some home businesses can be the ideal income-generator for a single parent family. If you are considering a home business, the following are some tips to get you started.

- **Assess your strengths and skills.** If you haven't already decided what to do, ask, "What do I enjoy most? What are my hobbies and interests?" "What skills have I acquired through volunteer work or jobs I've had?"

The following stories about two single parents who managed to support their children with a home business may inspire you to step out with your ideas.

*** SUSAN BRYG—SONLIGHT CLEANERS ***

After Susan's divorce, her income dropped drastically, even though she had a corporate job selling commercial real estate. Although her job had potential, for Susan, climbing the corporate ladder and single parenting didn't mix. It worried her that her daughters, who were first and third graders at the time, were staying at home alone until she arrived home—

sometimes after dark. Susan was usually numb and exhausted from stress by that time and had little energy for her daughters.

She decided to quit her corporate job and start a housecleaning service. In her area, the going rate for housecleaning services was $25 an hour at the time. Susan worked six hours a day, four days a week, and made $130 to $140 a day. She left for work when her girls left for school and was home when they returned in the afternoon or shortly thereafter. Within a month, Susan's schedule was full and she made more money housecleaning than working in commercial real estate. Her average income was $30,000 to $40,000 a year and included several "perks."

Because she was alone when she cleaned houses, she was able to listen to Christian radio all day and, by wearing a portable receiver, carried the music with her room to room and from house to house. She had low start-up expenses, and what she spent on the supplies and transportation could be deducted from her taxes. Plus, if one of her girls needed her because of illness, her customers understood and let her reschedule.

GREAT IDEAS FOR HOME BUSINESSES

- Plumbing, electrical, or heating and air conditioning services
- Providing day care
- Sewing, alterations, tailoring
- Housecleaning service
- Teaching cooking, music, or art
- Word processing and desk-top publishing, writing, editing
- Consulting (business or beauty)
- Marketing: selling clothes, vacuum cleaners, family photos, or other products through sample sales or parties
- Cooking: catering, wedding and birthday cakes, cookies
- Making handcrafted furniture, shelves, birdhouses, wreaths, dolls, bears, pottery, ornaments
- Gardening: fresh and dried herbs or flowers, fruits or vegetables
- Making jams or jellies
- Bookkeeping and accounting
- Tutoring: computer skills, study skills, any school subject
- Decorating: home or business
- Repairing: home, auto, small appliances, or lawn mowers

"Sonlight Cleaners" services became a strong, steady source of income and, eventually, Susan expanded her business to include a professional organizing service for offices, closets, and homes.

Tips for Starting a Housecleaning Business

- Give your business a name and have business cards printed.
- Design and distribute a flyer that explains your service.
- Get a partner, if needed.
- For pricing information, call cleaning services in your area and ask what they would charge to clean your house? Ask how their prices vary for different size houses.

(Contact Susan Bryg for information that includes a training manual and suggestions on running a successful house cleaning service: 285 Old Tree Tr, Roswell, GA 30075.)

*** JUNE FINE—FINE TAILORING ***

When June Fine's daughter was five, she found she was spending too much time away from her at night—selling cosmetics. She prayed and asked God to show her how she could work an intense eight-hour day and be home with her daughter in the evening to watch her grow up.

Soon after that prayer, June was at a church dinner and overheard a conversation that a tailor shop wanted someone for sales. Having been raised with a needle and thread and having a strong background in sales, she thought, *I might enjoy doing that*, although it was a men's clothing business. June was hired and began cold-calling and setting up appointments for the custom tailoring shop. After training and two and one-half years of experience, she started her own custom tailoring business at home, "Fine Tailoring," which enabled her to support herself and her daughter and even put her daughter through private school and college.

June's secrets to success involve a strong sense of priorities: "My plan has always been Matthew 6:33, to 'seek first the kingdom of God and His righteousness.'"

By 7:30 A.M. she is up, dressed for work, has breakfast fixed, and ready for Bible reading and prayer. Then she works an energetic eight-hour day. At night she lists the "Six Most Important Things" to do the next day and numbers them by importance. She sets short-term, long-range, and daily goals.

Most of all, June treats her customers as she would like to be treated. She respects their preferences, assists in questions of style, and helps them to feel secure in their business appearance.

June ranks raising her daughter as the number one advantage of having her own business. "I picked up Casey after school at 3:00 and got to be a mom. I took her home and worked in my office until 5:30, while she did homework. I was here to guide and direct her, and that meant the world to me."

Action Point

If you are interested in starting a home business, it is recommended that you first assess your suitability.

_____ Are you a self-starter?

_____ Do you enjoy working independently?

_____ Are you organized and resourceful?

Assess your strengths and skills. What do you enjoy; what are your hobbies and interests?

_____

What skills have you acquired through work or volunteering?

Recommendations to help you get started:

- Learn all you can about the business from the library or others in the business.
- Check local zoning, tax, and legal regulations for small businesses.
- Contact the Small Business Administration for a free start-up packet.
- Start small; keep your expenses low.
- Spread the word with business cards, flyers, or through friends and relatives.

List two or three possibilities for your business, and how you will research them.

How much money would it take to start your home business?

How much money can you invest in a home business?

A WORD OF CAUTION

Maybe you've seen those tiny advertisements in newspapers or in the back of magazines: "Make big bucks at home stuffing envelopes." These come-ons usually ask you to send money for more information, but what you get back is a letter telling how you can set up a phony business like theirs. Scams like this have victimized one-third of all Americans and cost them over $40 billion annually.

In case you might be tempted by a great-sounding, get-rich-quick offer, while looking for a home business or working toward other career goals, first read about two of the scams and how to avoid them.

1. Marketing offers: If you are told you have been selected to participate in a market test of a new product before it goes on sale to the public, turn the salesperson down. Usually you are told you can keep the product, but you have to pay for

MAKING INCOME THROUGH A HOME BUSINESS

shipping, which can be as high as $99 for large items.

2. Work at home: Advertisements for this scam appear in magazines, with the claim that $500 to $1,000 can be made if you have a computer. You just have to send $50 for information or $1,000 for a computer. Don't! Instead, investigate what home business area your skills and experience would be suited for.

Remember, some people are not meant to operate a home business. The following chapter can help you decide the type of work you are suited for.

For more information about starting or developing a home business, consult the following books. (If your local library does not have them, most libraries will order them at no charge to you.)

Home Business Happiness: Secrets on Keeping the Family Ship Afloat from Entrepreneurs Who Made It, Cheri Fuller (Starburst Publishers 1996).

Working at Home: The Dream That's Becoming a Trend, Lindsey O'Conner (Harvest House Publishers 1990).

Homemade Business: A Woman's Step-by-Step Guide to Earning Money at Home, Donna Partow (Focus on the Family 1993).

Chapter 10

CAREER PLANNING

YOU ARE UNIQUELY DESIGNED BY GOD.

"Thou didst form my inward parts; Thou didst weave me in my mother's womb. I will give thanks to Thee, for I am fearfully and wonderfully made; wonderful are Thy works, and my soul knows it very well" (Psalm 139:13-14).

You are a unique creation.
God made you for a special purpose.

YOU HAVE BEEN GIVEN UNIQUE TALENTS FOR A PURPOSE.

"And since we have gifts that differ according to the grace given to us, let each exercise them accordingly: if prophecy, according to the proportion of his faith; if service, in his serving; or he who teaches, in his teaching; or he who exhorts, in his exhortation; he who gives, with liberality; he who leads, with diligence; he who shows mercy, with cheerfulness" (Romans 12:6-8).

God gave each of us unique talents to use—not waste.
God has designed each of us with talents and gifts for His service.

YOU MUST DEVELOP THOSE TALENTS FOR EXCELLENCE.

"Do you see a man skilled in his work? He will stand before kings; he will not stand before obscure men" (Proverbs 22:29).

You should do your work as if you are actually working for the Lord.
Using your God-given talents to their fullest will give you success and joy.
Using your talents in work is a form of worship to Him.

WORK IS A STAGE FOR YOUR HIGHER CALLING.

"Let your light shine before men in such a way that they may see your good works, and glorify your Father who is in heaven" (Matthew 5:16).

When you let your light shine, others will see Christ through you.
Work is an excellent place to be a witness.

HOW TO MAKE GOOD CAREER DECISIONS

Action Point

Determine your purpose in life. Your work should contribute to achieving your life's purpose. What do you want to accomplish with your life?

_____

_____

Learn about your natural patterns, which is a combination of your abilities, interests, personality, work priorities and values. _Your Career in Changing Times_ and _Finding the Career That Fits You_ by Lee Ellis and Larry Burkett (Moody Press), and _The PathFinder_ by Lee Ellis (CFC) will help you discover your patterns.
List your abilities, interests, priorities and values:

_____

_____

_____

Investigate several occupations that fit your pattern. Remember, you're trying to avoid the round-pet-in-the-square-hole syndrome. It takes time and hard work to find the right match.
List three occupations that fit your pattern.

_____

_____

Seek God's direction and confirmation as you explore various occupations and careers. Ask those that know you well for counsel and advice.
List the people you will ask for advice.

_____

_____

Develop a career destination plan; investigate educational and training choices.
List your educational and career goals.

_____

_____

List your financial plans for reaching those goals.

_____

_____

Never quit learning; continue to read, learn new skills, and take training courses. With more knowledge and skills, you'll be better equipped to compete in the job market. Refine your career as you go along. Prepare to move into new areas of work that suit your individual talents and personality. Be flexible and adapt to change.

"My first step in getting off welfare or any assistance was getting an education to secure my financial independence and provide for my children," said one single parent. When she found the right community college program for the job skills she needed, this woman received a child care scholarship, a tuition scholarship, and a book scholarship. With these scholarships, she was able to secure an Associate of Arts degree in word-information processing and land a much better paying job.

If furthering your education will help you meet your career goal, there are many local scholarships, federal work-study programs, grants, and other opportunities available. Often an employer has set aside funds for continuing education of employees. With the financial aid information in Chapter 12, seek God's guidance, get some career counsel, and set your goals!

> THERE NEVER HAS BEEN a get-rich-quick scheme that didn't sound terrific on the surface. Promoters are better at disguising the bad deals than most people are at detecting the good ones. Every year Christians risk and lose money they can not afford to lose while seeking that "big deal." Can it be avoided? Most certainly, but not on the basis of human wisdom.

Get-Rich-Quick Schemes usually are ones that offer an excessive gain for little or no apparent risk. The following are some basic principles for how to avoid get-rich-quick schemes.

- Stick with what you know.
- Don't risk borrowed money.
- Buy investments with utility.
- Don't make quick decisions.
- And seek good counsel!

SINGLE PARENTS
AND THE LOCAL CHURCH

Imagine you are walking along a beach and you see a woman flailing in the water. As you draw closer and peer toward the churning waves, you see her head go under. You stand there, transfixed, wondering if you just imagined it all.

But then she surfaces; she gasps for air, and the agony on her face is apparent. She tries to call for help but the undercurrent attacks, and before you see her again she sinks below the surface. This continues and you see her grow weaker and weaker until, finally, she disappears.

On a daily basis, the number of single parents continues to grow to staggering numbers. Many of them find it difficult, even impossible, to "keep their heads above water" and are drowning in the cares that are associated with being single parents.

Anyone who has been a parent knows how difficult it is to "juggle all the balls in the air" at once, even when there are four hands of two committed parents doing the "juggling." In the case of a single parent, the same balls have to be juggled; however, two of the hands are missing.

Until we have walked in someone else's shoes, we cannot possibly understand the needs of that person. Does that mean we simply do nothing to help single parents? The church can make a difference in the lives of single parents and in the lives of their children.

In sales there is a principle called "The Law of 200." Simply put, it says that at any given moment, each of us has at least 200 people in our circle of influence. One or more of those 200 people in your circle—and very likely, in your church—is "drowning."[1] Anything, no matter how small, can make a significant difference.

Single parents seeking financial counsel generally don't want to turn to the government to meet their needs. They want answers and guidance. Unfortunately many churches will send them to welfare, or bankruptcy court, instead of meeting their needs.

These churches fear that if they help one needy family they will be inundated with needs they can't meet, but that has been proved to be a false assumption. Studies have shown that to be successful single parents need to be surrounded with practical and financial assistance, if they have low incomes, and with ongoing spiritual and emotional support. This support provides them with a sense of community and connection. And, churches that provide these things find their membership and financial support actually increase, because believers who join them strengthen these efforts.

Some churches believe that helping those in need takes away from God's work in the lives of the needy, when the opposite has proved to be true. God works through people. To keep a healthy balance, the church must learn to tell the difference between helping and enabling. Many low-income families want to learn how to move beyond dependence. And when undeserved favor is given, along with accountability, guidance, and support, many of these families turn their hearts toward God and give back much more to help others in need than they receive. These churches see the results of their outreach in the changed lives of single parent families.

Our research shows that most churches want to do something; they just don't know where to begin. The single parent department of Christian Financial Concepts assists churches by training them to develop ministries that meet the practical needs of single parents. If your church is interested in doing something more for single parents, send your church's name, a contact name, and the church's address to CFC's single parent department at PO Box 2377, Gainesville, GA 30503-2377.

The following are a few ways you can creatively and compassionately show you care enough to help a single parent.

Individual Acts of Kindness
- Write a note of encouragement. It's amazing how fantastic it is to open the mailbox and, instead of seeing a bill, get a note full of grace and encouragement.

- Offer to care for a single parent's children. Everyone needs a break from children once in a while, and children need to learn to respect a number of different authority figures.

- Invite a single parent family to your home for meals. Though offering hospitality to them during the holidays is needed, single parents need meals, caring, and fellowship throughout the year.

- Offer to coach youth sports. Whether you are the coach or a parent with a child on the team, invite a child from a single parent family to be on the team, and offer to transport the children of single parents if possible.

- If you are good with cars, offer to change the oil and fix minor automotive problems. Most single parents don't have the finances to replace cars or pay for the routine upkeep on the vehicles they have.

- Although food warehouses continue to grow in popularity, such large quantities often are not appropriate for most single parent families. Offer to take a single parent shopping and go in together to split the cost of large items. Another solution is to buy an item, divide it in half, and offer half to the single parent.

- Sometimes the exhaustion of single parenting puts a person into automatic pilot, without the energy to think of fun activities to do with children. Purchase inexpensive kites, pack a picnic, bring the family over on a weekend day, and help them to have fun.

- When you make a meal that can be frozen and reheated, consider making a double portion. Offer it to a single parent to put in the freezer for a hectic day.

- Listen. Sometimes just a sympathetic ear or a shoulder to cry on is what is needed. While listening, be sure you keep the details confidential.

- Giving away outgrown children's clothing is a natural and is much appreciated. However, when does the single parent ever get something new? Parents put themselves last to provide for their children's needs. If you can't buy new clothes for a single parent, why not go through your closet and choose a few items you rarely, if ever, wear and offer them to a single parent friend of the same size. The blessing it brings will be well worth the time it takes to glean items from your wardrobe.

- Cameras, film, and developing costs usually are not in the single parent's budget. Yet precious memories of growing children need to be preserved. Purchase an inexpensive camera and film, plus a gift certificate for developing costs, and give them to a single parent.

- Don't be judgmental. Regardless of how a person became a single parent, that person needs your support and encouragement—not criticism. Your place should be building up the single parent—not condemning that person.

- Sort through toys and books in good condition and offer them to a single parent family. Even very young children can learn from giving away a special toy to someone.

- When you rent videos, offer them to a single parent while there is still time left on the rental. That way, they have approximately two hours of free entertainment at no extra cost to you!

- Small kindnesses like flowers from your garden, a homemade dessert, or an encouraging phone call can go a long way toward preserving sanity.

- Most of all, take the initiative to offer your friendship. With all the rigors of work and the responsibilities of home and family, many single parents don't have the time to nurture and develop relationships they need with other adults. Take the initiative. Call and offer kind words of love and encouragement. It could be a wonderful new friendship that will last for a lifetime.

How Churches Can Help Single Parents
- Start a once-a-month car care ministry.
- Give single parents a gift subscription to the *Single-Parent Family* magazine (Focus on the Family, Colorado Spring, CO); the *Christian Single* magazine (Lifeway Press, Nashville, TN); or the Dear Dad newsletter for single fathers (Parenting at Their Best, Colorado Springs, CO).

- Offer child care free or at low cost for single parents who work.
- Provide financial counseling, both short-term and long-term.
- Have a Clothes Closet ministry and/or a church-wide "swap meet" to assist single parents in meeting their clothing needs.
- Start a mentoring program or a support group for single parents. A loving, trusted mentor (an older person) or a couple to befriend the single parent can be a life-saver, especially during the first year as a single parent, which is by far the worst.

> God wants the best of what we have—not the leftovers. God does not want us to give our worn-out clothes, broken lawn mowers, or beat-up cars to the people in our midst who have needs. God wants us to fill the needs of others with our best.

- Children from single parent families need exposure to families and missing parent role models. Positive role models can change children's lives. They need men and women who are willing to participate in their lives—as teachers, troop leaders, or someone who just notices them and talks to them at church or during church activities. This is just as important for girls as it is for boys.

  Churches offering this kind of mentoring suggest you make sure the environment is safe and activities are in groups, not individually, unless the mentor has proven character. It's unfortunate that it has come to this when dealing with Christians, but some churches have found it necessary to investigate anyone who wants to work with children, male and female.

- Include single parents in adult activities and seasonal celebrations at the church. People can offer to provide transportation or help with child care (or child care costs) so single parents can attend church events and fellowship events.
- As service projects, men and women from the adult and youth groups can help single parents with mowing and yard jobs, washing cars, washing windows, and baby sitting on Saturdays.
- Churches need to make married couples aware of the loneliness single parents can experience during the holidays and on Sunday afternoons. "I remember when Heidi and I first moved to a new area and didn't have anyone to share Sunday dinner with," said one single parent. Most of the time they could handle being alone, but on Mother's Day or Father's Day the need for fellowship is great. Holidays are tough for single parents. It makes a world of difference to be included.

These are just a few ways you can aid a family. You see, when you help a single parent, you offer relief to an entire family and make a significant difference in their emotional, spiritual, and physical health.

You also are being obedient to God, because He commands the local church to care for the widows and orphans. *This is pure and undefiled religion in the sight of our God and*

Father, to visit orphans and widows in their distress, and to keep oneself unstained by the world" (James 1:27).

As much or more than anyone else in our society, single parents and their children need support and help—not from the federal government but from the body of Christ, as God's hand of love extended.

One Sunday after early morning church, Monique, a single mother, was walking out of the church with her two year old beside her. She was exhausted. She had been working eleven-hour days and had worked eight hours that Saturday. Her daughter wanted her and this mom had nothing left to give. Monique was at the end of her rope and just needed some time to sleep and re-group. She didn't tell anyone that; she just prayed for God's help.

While walking out of the church, she passed a lady who was in church all the time. She looked at Monique and said, "Would you like me to take Heidi for the afternoon? You look like you need a break." It was the best thing anyone could have done for this exhausted mom. She just needed a break—one she didn't have to pay for and one she didn't have to worry about.

We can individually, and as a church, be the answer to a single parent or a child's prayer. God will be glorified by our service, and we'll be blessed.

CFC has designed a training program to teach churches how to establish a single parent ministry that helps single parents meet their practical needs. For information on seminar schedules, call CFC at 770-534-1000.

---

1. Adapted from *Please Help Me, I'm Drowning*, Carmen Leal-Pock. Used by permission.

Chapter 12

FINANCIAL AID FOR EDUCATION

The term *financial aid* refers to the sources of help that are available to meet educational costs. Most single parents immediately assume they cannot afford to go to technical school or college or provide private or Christian schooling for their children. They don't realize that financial aid is available at many schools to pay for education. The only way to know if financial aid is available, or if your family is eligible, is to apply. However, the following are some factors to keep in mind.

- Many private, parochial, and Christian schools have scholarship funding available for deserving students. Contact those in your community.
- Most financial aid is awarded on the basis of need.
- The "need" is the difference between what it costs to attend a particular private school and what you can afford to pay.
- Since your income may be low, your need may be greater.
- You or your child could be eligible for different amounts of scholarship aid at different schools.
- Academic performance or special abilities are considered sometimes, in addition to need.
- Financial aid may include a work-study program, in which students perform services for the school either in the summer or before or after the day's classes during the school term.

Applying for Financial Aid

First, fill out the school's Financial Aid Form and turn it in before the deadline for

THE FINANCIAL GUIDE FOR THE SINGLE PARENT WORKBOOK

the best opportunity to receive funds. The form is then sent to the School Scholarship Service in Princeton, New Jersey. Based on the information provided on the form, the school or School Scholarship Service will determine what you can afford to pay for your child's schooling; this is called the "Expected Family Contribution." Factors considered are the family's income and the number of children in private school and college.

The school or the School Scholarship Service may need to look at your previous year's tax return, plus any extenuating circumstance, to decide on the amount of financial aid to award.

If you have unusual personal or financial circumstances that don't appear in the numbers but affect your family's ability to pay for education (such as high medical expenses or disability), write a letter. Explain in detail your financial situation and note any special circumstances.

How to Pay for a College Education (Yours or Your Children's)

There are several options for financing a college or vo-tech (vocational-technical) education. Most people will use a combination of the options described below during their school years. Obviously, cost will be a major criterion in selecting the school you or your children will attend, but we encourage you to investigate all the possibilities before you decide you can't afford a school you really want to attend—and one that meets your educational or training goals.

The following are available plans for financing education.

- **Work-study programs.** Most college students work to pay part of their expenses. These programs:
   1. do not have to be paid back.
   2. offer work experience.
   3. reduce tuition expenses.

They work well for students:
   1. who live in campus housing or with relatives.
   2. who do not have other expenses.
   3. who have financial assistance from family.

They do not work well for:
   1. single parents who need an income while they are attending school.

- **Parents and other family help.**
   1. Consider your ability and willingness to finance all of part of your child's education. Investing small amounts while your child is young will help tremendously.
   2. Find out if your family is willing or able to help finance part of your tuition or help with other expenses, such as child care.

- **Grants or scholarships.**
  1. *State Educational Grants* are issued through colleges, based on need.
  2. *The Federal Pell Grant* is federal money sent to colleges and then distributed to students. Need is assessed by using a government formula.
  3. *The Federal Work-Study Program (FWSP)* is a federal sponsored program that funds jobs for college students to pay tuition, usually on campus.
  4. *Scholarships: See other sources listed below.*

- **Loans. Use as a last resort.** These funds have to be paid back at a later date.
  1. In most situations you can find a way to finance your education without a loan.
  2. If you do decide you have to have a student loan:
     a. Borrow only what you absolutely need at the lowest student loan rate.
     b. Borrow for a short period of time, if possible. Most lenders allow students to finish school before repaying loans.
     c. Pay it back as quickly as possible.
     d. Sacrifice as needed to get out of debt.

Other Sources of College Aid Information
- High school counselor
- College financial aid officer
- Library
- Your pastor
- Your employer or parent's employer
- Service organizations
- Educational opportunities office
- United States Armed Forces

(Adapted from *How to Pay for Your Education: Financial Aid* by Lee Ellis, Career Pathways, Gainesville, Georgia)

Action Point

After exploring the financial aid options, determine which ones most fit your situation and goals. List your options here.

_____

_____

_____

Chapter 13

GOD WORKS THROUGH OUR FINANCES[1]

Scripture makes it clear that God works through our finances to guide us, mold our attitudes, increase our faith, and help us conform to His will for our lives.

1. God will use money to strengthen our trust in Him. It is often through money that God can clearly and objectively show us that He is God and in control of everything. Jesus reminded His followers, *"Your heavenly Father knows that you need all these things. But seek first His kingdom and His righteousness; and all these things shall be added to you"* (Matthew 6:32-33). This principle establishes that God will use money to strengthen our trust if we will just accept our positions as stewards and turn it over to Him.

2. God will use money to develop our trustworthiness. This principle is important because our lives revolve around making money, spending money, saving money, and giving money. God gauges our ability to handle spiritual "riches" by our stewardship of material wealth. *"If therefore you have not been faithful in the use of unrighteous mammon, who will entrust the true riches to you?"* (Luke 16:11).

3. God will use money to prove His love. Many Christians remain outside God's will because they are afraid to yield their lives and their resources to Him. Matthew 7:11 has the answer: *"If you then, being evil, know how to give good gifts to your children, how much more shall your Father who is in heaven give what is good to those who ask Him!"* In other words, Jesus is saying that God assumes the responsibility of providing the basic necessities for everyone who trusts in Him.

4. God will use money to demonstrate His power over this world. Too often we forget that we worship the Creator of the universe. We tend to think of God in human terms and relate to Him as we relate to a human. It is important that we understand God's power and His resources. As God gives us small things, our confidence begins to grow; and the more our confidence in Him grows, the more He is able to supply. Thus God can use money to demonstrate His power to us. *"For the Scripture says, 'Whoever believes in Him will not be disappointed.' For there is no distinction between Jew and Greek; for the same Lord is Lord of all, abounding in riches for all who call upon Him"* (Romans 10:11-12).

5. God will use money to unite Christians through many shared blessings. *"He who gathered much did not have too much, and he who gathered little had no lack"* (2 Corinthians 8:15). God will use the abundance of one Christian to supply the needs of another. Later He may reverse the relationship, as described in 2 Corinthians 8:14: *"At this present time your abundance being a supply for their want, that their abundance also may become a supply for your want, that there may be equality."* It is important, as we face times of economic chaos, that Christians accept the principle that a surplus of money in our lives, indeed everything we have, is there for a purpose.

6. God will use money to provide direction for our lives. There is probably no way God can direct our lives faster than through the abundance or lack of money. Too often we believe God will direct our lives only through abundance of money, and we keep probing to see where He supplies it. However, God can steer us along His path through the *lack* of money just as quickly. *"And let us not lose heart in doing good, for in due time we shall reap if we do not grow weary"* (Galatians 6:9). We don't give up just because we face some difficulty. God will ultimately supply the direction we are seeking, and one of the primary ways He gives insight into His will is by providing or withholding money. Christians seeking God's will must be certain that they have first relinquished control of their lives, including finances, and are truly seeking God's direction.

7. God can use money to satisfy the needs of others. Christians who hoard money and never plan for their financial lives cannot experience this area of fulfillment. Often I hear Christians say, "How can I give? I barely have enough to meet my needs now." If we have never learned to give, God can never give back. God cannot be in control as long as we believe we are the owners. *"Give, and it will be given to you; good measure, pressed down, shaken together, running over, they will pour into your lap. For by your standard of measure it will be measured to you in return"* (Luke 6:38).

Once we realize that God is truly in control, we can learn to be content and dedicate ourselves to serving Him. *"Let us also lay aside every encumbrance, and the sin which so easily entangles us, and let us run with endurance the race that is set before us"* (Hebrews 12:1).

---

1. "Money Sense" by Larry Burkett, *Moody* magazine, October 1995. (Adapted in part from *Your Finances in Changing Times,* Moody Press.)

Appendix

FORMS

MONTHLY INCOME & EXPENSES

GROSS INCOME PER MONTH _____

    Salary _____

    Interest _____

    Dividends _____

    Other _____

LESS:

  1. Tithe _____

  2. Tax (Est. - Incl. Fed., State, FICA) _____

    NET SPENDABLE INCOME _____

  3. Housing _____

    Mortgage (rent) _____

    Insurance _____

    Taxes _____

    Electricity _____

    Gas _____

    Water _____

    Sanitation _____

    Telephone _____

    Maintenance _____

    Other _____

  4. Food _____

  5. Automobile(s) _____

    Payments _____

    Gas & Oil _____

    Insurance _____

    License/Taxes _____

    Maint./Repair/Replace _____

  6. Insurance _____

    Life _____

    Medical _____

    Other _____

  7. Debts _____

    Credit Card _____

    Loans & Notes _____

    Other _____

  8. Enter. & Recreation _____

    Eating Out _____

    Baby Sitters _____

    Activities/Trips _____

    Vacation _____

    Other _____

  9. Clothing _____

  10. Savings _____

  11. Medical Expenses _____

    Doctor _____

    Dentist _____

    Drugs _____

    Other _____

  12. Miscellaneous _____

    Toiletry, cosmetics _____

    Beauty, barber _____

    Laundry, cleaning _____

    Allowances, lunches _____

    Subscriptions _____

    Gifts (incl. Christmas) _____

    Cash _____

    Other _____

  13. School/Child Care _____

    Tuition _____

    Materials _____

    Transportation _____

    Day Care _____

  14. Investments _____

    TOTAL EXPENSES _____

  INCOME VS. EXPENSES

    Net Spendable Income _____

    Less Expenses _____

  15. Unallocated Surplus Income [1] _____

[1] This category is used when extra unbudgeted money is received, which would be kept in the checking account to be used within a few weeks; otherwise, it should be transferred to a budgeted category.

FORM 1

VARIABLE EXPENSE PLANNING

Plan for those expenses that are not paid on a regular monthly basis by estimating the yearly cost and determining the monthly amount needed to be set aside for that expense. A helpful formula is to allow the previous year's expense and add 5 percent.

	Estimated Cost	**Per Month**
1. VACATION	$ _____ ÷ 12 =	$ _____
2. DENTIST	$ _____ ÷ 12 =	$ _____
3. DOCTOR	$ _____ ÷ 12 =	$ _____
4. AUTOMOBILE	$ _____ ÷ 12 =	$ _____
5. ANNUAL INSURANCE	$ _____ ÷ 12 =	$ _____
(Life)	($ _____ ÷ 12 =	$ _____)
(Medical)	($ _____ ÷ 12 =	$ _____)
(Auto)	($ _____ ÷ 12 =	$ _____)
(Home)	($ _____ ÷ 12 =	$ _____)
6. CLOTHING	$ _____ ÷ 12 =	$ _____
7. INVESTMENTS	$ _____ ÷ 12 =	$ _____
8. OTHER	$ _____ ÷ 12 =	$ _____
	$ _____ ÷ 12 =	$ _____

FORM 2

BUDGET PERCENTAGE GUIDELINES

Gross Income Per Month   _____

1.	Tithe	(___ % of Gross)	= $ _____
2.	Tax	(___ % of Gross)	= $ _____

Net Spendable Income

3.	Housing	(___ % of Net)	= $ _____
4.	Food	(___ % of Net)	= $ _____
5.	Auto	(___ % of Net)	= $ _____
6.	Insurance	(___ % of Net)	= $ _____
7.	Debts	(___ % of Net)	= $ _____
8.	Entertain. & Rec.	(___ % of Net)	= $ _____
9.	Clothing	(___ % of Net)	= $ _____
10.	Savings	(___ % of Net)	= $ _____
11.	Medical	(___ % of Net)	= $ _____
12.	Miscellaneous	(___ % of Net)	= $ _____
13.	Investments	(___ % of Net)	= $ _____
14.	School/ Child Care	(___ % of Net)	= $ _____
15.	Alimony/ Child Support	(___ % of Net)	= $ _____
Total	**(Cannot exceed Net Spendable Income)**		$ _____
16.	Unallocated Surplus Income	=	$ _____

To figure the dollar amount for each category, multiply the percent by your gross or net income as indicated. Be sure to put a decimal in front of the percent number before multiplying. The following example uses a gross income of $1250 per month, multiplied by 10 percent for tithe and a net income of $875 multiplied by 40 percent for housing.

Example: Tithe   .10(%) x Gross $1250 = $125

                   Housing .40(%) x Net $ 875 = $350

Refer to page 43 for percentage guidelines.

FORM 3

BUDGET ANALYSIS

PER YEAR _____   NET SPENDABLE INCOME PER MONTH _____

PER MONTH _____

MONTHLY PAYMENT CATEGORY	EXISTING BUDGET	MONTHLY GUIDELINE BUDGET	DIFFERENCE + OR -	NEW MONTHLY BUDGET
1. Tithe				
2. Taxes				
NET SPENDABLE INCOME (Per Month)	$_____	$_____	$_____	$_____
3. Housing				
4. Food				
5. Automobiles(s)				
6. Insurance				
7. Debts				
8. Enter. & Recreation				
9. Clothing				
10. Savings				
11. Medical				
12. Miscellaneous				
13. School/Child Care				
14. Investments				
TOTALS (Items 3-14)	$_____	$_____	✕	$_____
15. Unallocated Surplus Income				

FORM 4

INCOME ALLOCATION

		INCOME SOURCE/PAY PERIOD			
INCOME					
BUDGET CATEGORY	**MONTHLY ALLOCATION**				
1. Tithe					
2. Tax					
3. Housing					
4. Food					
5. Auto					
6. Insurance					
7. Debts					
8. Entertainment & Recreation					
9. Clothing					
10. Savings					
11. Medical/Dental					
12. Miscellaneous					
13. School/Child Care					
14. Investments					
15. Unallocated Surplus Income					

FORM 5

SAVINGS ACCOUNT ALLOCATIONS

Date	Deposit	With-drawal	Balance	Housing	Food	Auto Insur.	Auto Maint.	Insur-ance	Clothes	Medical					

FORM 6

101

INDIVIDUAL ACCOUNT PAGE

_____ $ _____ $ _____
ACCOUNT CATEGORY   ALLOCATION   ALLOCATION

DATE	TRANSACTION	DEPOSIT	WITHDRAWAL	BALANCE

FORM 7

CHECKBOOK LEDGER

DATE	CK. #	TRANSACTION	DEPOSIT	WITHDRAWAL	BALANCE

FORM 7a

LIST OF DEBTS

as of _____

TO WHOM OWED	CONTACT NAME PHONE NO.	PAY OFF	PAYMENTS LEFT	MONTHLY PAYMENT	DATE

FORM 8

104

Larry Burkett, founder and president of Christian Financial Concepts, is the best-selling author of 47 books on business and personal finances and two novels. He also hosts two radio programs broadcast on hundreds of stations worldwide.

Larry holds degrees in marketing and finance, and for several years served as a manager in the space program at Cape Canaveral, Florida. He also has been vice president of an electronics manufacturing firm. Larry's education, business experience, and solid understanding of God's Word enable him to give practical, Bible-based financial counsel to families, churches, and businesses.

Founded in 1976, Christian Financial Concepts is a nonprofit, nondenominational ministry dedicated to helping God's people gain a clear understanding of how to manage their money according to scriptural principles. While practical assistance is provided on many levels, the purpose of CFC is simply *to bring glory to God by freeing His people from financial bondage so they may serve Him to their utmost.*

One major avenue of ministry involves the training of volunteers in budget and debt counseling and linking them with financially troubled families and individuals through a nationwide referral network. CFC also provides financial management seminars and workshops for churches and other groups. (Formats available include audio, video, video with moderator, and live instruction.) A full line of printed and audio-visual materials related to money management is available through CFC's materials department (1-800-722-1976).

Career Pathways, another outreach of Christian Financial Concepts, helps teenagers and adults find their occupational calling. The Career Pathways "Assessment" gauges a person's work priorities, skills, vocational interests, and personality. Reports in each of these areas define a person's strengths, weaknesses, and unique, God-given pattern for work.

For further information about the ministry of Christian Financial Concepts, write to:

Christian Financial Concepts
PO Box 2458
Gainesville, Georgia 30503-2458